COUNTRY SOLOS
for Guitar

by
Steve Trovato

PLAYBACK+
Speed • Pitch • Balance • Loop

To access audio visit:
www.halleonard.com/mylibrary

Enter Code
2864-8311-2245-5234

Additional Editing by Adam St. James

ISBN 978-0-634-01392-8

HAL•LEONARD®

7777 W. BLUEMOUND RD. P.O. BOX 13819 MILWAUKEE, WI 53213

Visit Hal Leonard Online at
www.halleonard.com

Table of Contents

Introduction

Hello, and welcome to ProLicks *Country Solos for Guitar.* In the pages of this book, I'm going to walk you through classic country rhythm and lead patterns as played in the audio examples. In Chapter 1, "Hot Banjo Rolls," I'll show you one of the essential fingerpicking techniques in country music. It's a great place to begin your exploration of country and country rock guitar playing. Later in the book, we'll explore varying styles that will give you a solid foundation in country lead and rhythm guitar playing. I'll explain the key techniques and solo phrases in country styles based on Chet Atkins and Jerry Reed-style fingerpicking, Albert Lee and Steve Morse-style chicken pickin', hot double stops, open-string licks, and great steel-guitar licks you can play on your six-string. You'll be able to listen to me solo in all those styles on the accompanying audio, then I'll dissect each and every note so that you can master these styles as well.

How to Use This Book

In laying out solos in each of these six country styles, it turns out that there are a lot of short phrases that you can learn, lift out, and use in your own style of playing. In other words, you don't have to learn each solo exactly the way it was played on the track. You can listen through all the tracks, hear everything that I'm going to play for you, then go back and pick out the phrases that you like best. Then you can learn those phrases and incorporate them into your own style of playing. It's good practice to take all of these ideas and mix them in with what you already know how to play.

Of course, there are things to be learned by playing an entire solo: how the solo builds, how to make a transition from one chorus to the next, how to begin and end the whole thing. Those are elements of style that make the phrases fit together so that they actually sound good. But the individual phrases themselves can be picked out and used in practically any country solo. With a little tweaking, these phrases can also be used in songs with different tempos and in different keys.

In addition to performing the six complete solos, I'm going to explain each phrase individually using "Practice Points" and detailed directions that will help you duplicate my solo phrases. Through these Practice Points, I'll tell you all about the left hand, the right hand, different little tricks, techniques, and where to place your hand on the neck. Read the musical notation and tablature for each phrase as you listen to the track, refer to the Practice Points that explain the details of each phrase, then practice along with my audio examples.

When we get through, you'll know all the phrases, and you can play them along with the full band, rhythm-only tracks immediately after each solo. Playing along with the rhythm-only tracks will give you an opportunity to get a feel for how your phrasing sounds against a rhythm section and whether or not you're playing correctly. Some of the phrases are easier than others. Some are slower; some are faster. Take your time. Practice each phrase as many times as you need to get it right. And most of all, have fun!

Remember, take these licks one at a time. Some of them only work over one of the chords in the progression, or in a certain situation. Some of them can be laid over any of the chords. You have to experiment a little bit to see what you can do with them once you get them down. But these are all real solid, traditional, classic licks, and I think once you integrate them into your style, you'll have a lot of fun developing them.

Before You Begin

Since we're doing a lot of string bending, it would be very helpful if you would use lighter-gauge strings on your guitar, namely a set that's gauged with a nine (.009) or a ten (.010) on top. Those will work pretty well. If you use an eleven (.011) or twelve (.012) or anything above, you might find that there's too much resistance to bend the notes up to pitch. There's a couple of really big string bends in some of the chapters, and it takes me all of my effort to get the notes up to pitch. So you'll want to use a relatively light gauge.

Get In Tune

First things first: Play Track 13 and tune your guitar to mine. That way, you can play along with the audio and sound great.

Recording Credits

John Shank, engineer
Steve Trovato, lead guitar
Keith Wyatt, rhythm guitar

Tim Emmons, bass
Jack Dukes, drums

1 Hot Banjo Rolls

The banjo licks you'll hear in the solo "Hot Banjo Rolls" involve a technique that's highly sought after. People are always asking me about them. They're played by several top country pickers: Albert Lee, Jerry Reed, Ray Flacke, James Burton, and Chet Atkins, just to mention a few.

It can be hard trying to figure out these kinds of licks off a record because they're usually going by so fast, and they're played so fast, that they're over before you figure out more than a couple of notes. So we're going to slow them down and analyzie them. We're going to take each one and break it down to its nuts and bolts. Then we're going to put them together, play a standard country progression, and create a solo using just these banjo rolls. The technique requires a lot of practice and patience before it can be worked up to a tempo at which it sounds good.

The Proper Tone

When I recorded this solo with the band, I used my '61 Strat, through a pedal board into a Peavey Special 130. For the sound I got, I had on the treble pickup. It's a stock Strat pickup. For the main portion of the tune, the melody, I played through a compressor and a Boss digital delay pedal.

Hot Banjo Rolls

full band minus guitar

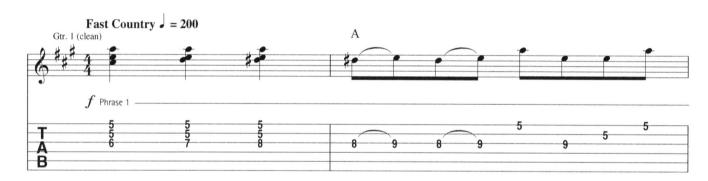

Right Hand Technique

As in bluegrass banjo, most of the work is done with the right hand. The way I do it on the track, I don't use a thumbpick. I've developed a style using a regular standard pick and the middle and ring fingers of my right hand to create the three-pick sound you hear in bluegrass banjo. With bluegrass banjo, most of the guys use a thumbpick and two metal fingerpicks. I've found that I can't do that on guitar because I couldn't play the fast note lines that I needed to play without switching picking styles. So I've developed this style.

When you hear guys such as Chet Atkins and Jerry Reed do this, they're using a thumbpick and the index and middle fingers of their right hand. When you hear guys such as Ray Flacke, Albert Lee, and myself use this kind of technique, we're using a pick, middle, and ring fingers of the right hand.

A basic problem when using a pick and two fingers is that if you have no fingernails on the middle and ring fingers of your right hand, they don't have that crisp attack on the strings that the pick has. So when you play three consecutive notes using your pick, middle, and ring fingers, the pick is going to have a sharp attack on your strings, and then your two fingers are just going to sound like two thumbs. The idea is to grow your fingernails just slightly—I would say a sixteenth of an inch, just slightly longer than you would normally keep them if you didn't need them to play guitar. I keep mine about a sixteenth of an inch long, and I put some clear nail hardener on them. I learned that from Albert Lee. That keeps them from wearing down; metal strings will wear down your fingernails in no time, because the string is just plain harder than the fingernail. This clear polish seems to work.

Looking at my right hand, if I place my fingers on the strings of my guitar, I'm going to play at a slight angle. Normally I would keep my wrist straight, but when I play this banjo-roll style I'm going to tilt my wrist slightly down. I place the pick flat on the string, let's say the sixth string, then I start to turn it down at an angle, like I'm turning a key in a lock, until it falls off the string. That's the angle I want it to be at: tilted. When I have my pick tilted like that, my middle and ring fingers will be in a position to pull straight up against the strings, rather than pulling back on them as if I had the pick flat against the strings. So this forces me to angle my wrist down a little bit. That's the correct hand position for these banjo rolls.

A Simple Exercise

Before we can achieve any kind of technique or speed, we'll have to train our hands to play basic forward and backward banjo rolls. Figure 1 is a simple exercise that I've designed to help you develop your right-hand rolls. I've taken a standard six-string E chord in the first position—a regular old E chord—and I play consecutive sets of three strings starting on the sixth string.

I don't use any kind of an anchor when I play these rolls. My right hand is not resting anywhere on the guitar at all for this particular technique. The way I'm moving my hand down across the strings is to move my elbow. It's not a wrist movement; it's an elbow movement. My wrist is staying at the same angle. I'm just lowering my elbow a little bit each time.

Figure 1: The Forward Roll

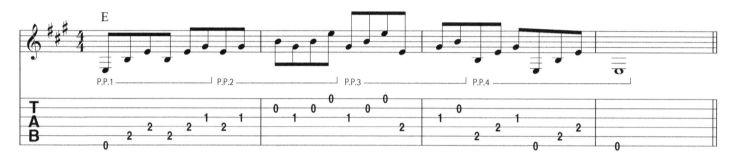

Practice Point 1: I'm not playing all the strings with my pick. I play the lowest of the three strings in each set with my pick, the middle string with my middle finger, and the highest string in each set of three strings with my ring finger. So it's a forward roll. I think of it as "pick, two, three." You want to concentrate on getting a snap out of all three strings. I play strings 6, 5, and 4; then move my right hand down and play 5, 4, 3.

Practice Point 2: Then I move my hand down again and play 4, 3, 2; then I move it down again and play 3, 2, 1.

Practice Point 3: You need to develop this technique both descending and ascending across the strings. So go down three strings at a time, then start the same thing and come back up the strings. Play 3, 2, 1; then 4, 3, 2.

Practice Point 4: Then play 5, 4, 3; and finally 6, 5, 4. Just go back and forth like that.

This style needs to be played very evenly. It's going to take some training and some patience. Don't try to do it fast; keep it slow. Speed is a by-product of accuracy. You don't learn how to play fast by practicing fast, you learn how to play fast by practicing accurately, slowly—and not making mistakes.

Eventually you'll work this up to a faster tempo. If you were sitting here with me, I would demand that you use a metronome. I don't believe in practicing anything on guitar without a metronome. So if you do have a metronome, I would suggest you use it, because you want to get even spacing between each one of these triplets. The best way to do that is to use a metronome.

After you've worked these rolls out slowly, you'll start to increase the tempo. We have to get these going at a rather brisk tempo, but most of the work is done with the right hand. You want to get these banjo rolls going at about 160 beats per minute.

Exercise 2: The Reverse Roll

Reverse rolls are a lot tougher. I'm not going to focus on reverse rolls in this book, but let me suggest a practice exercise that will help you incorporate reverse rolls into your playing.

Figure 2: The Reverse Roll

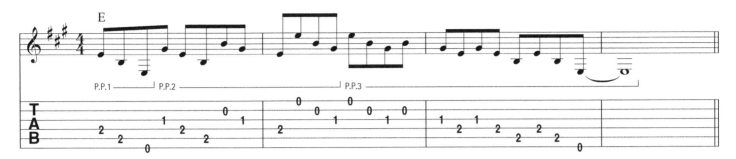

Practice Point 1: Take the same E chord, but start with the ring finger of your right hand, rather than the pick, and play backwards: ring finger, middle finger, pick. The ring finger and middle finger are upstrokes, and the pick is a downstroke. Play it with the same rhythm, but play it backwards. Start with the fourth string, and play 4, 5, 6.

Practice Point 2: Then play 3, 4, 5; then 2, 3, 4; then 1, 2, 3.

Practice Point 3: To descend play 1, 2, 3; 2, 3, 4; 3, 4, 5; 4, 5, 6.

A Different Kind of Roll

The next step is to take these arpeggio rolls a step further. This time, I play A triads all the way up the fingerboard. This is a flashy lick that I find myself using from time to time.

Figure 3: Triad Rolls

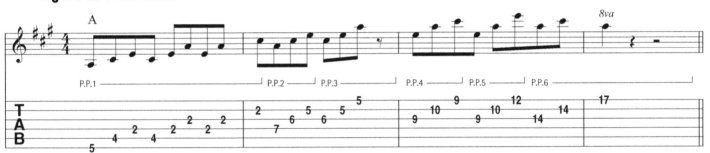

Practice Point 1: I start this practice exercise in 2nd position, with my fourth finger on A at the 5th fret on the sixth string. Then I play C# with my third finger at the 4th fret on the fifth string. Then I barre across the 2nd fret on strings 4, 3, and 2 with my index finger.

Then I play my banjo roll, just like in Figure 1. You have to be able to switch the position of your left hand while maintaining the roll with your right hand. So I start by playing 6, 5, 4; then 5, 4, 3; then 4, 3, 2.

Practice Point 2: At that point I switch positions. I move my left hand up to 5th position and play an A triad in the fifth position. I put my third finger on A at the 7th fret on the fourth string, play C# at the 6th fret on the third string with my second finger, and then E at the 5th fret on the second string with my first finger. So I pick 4, 3, 2.

Practice Point 3: Then I move down a set of strings and play C#, E, and then A at the 5th fret on the first string with my first finger, which I barre across the 5th fret on the first and second strings. It's just an A chord on the top four strings. I pick three, two, one. So I started with an A triad on the sixth string and wound up all the way on the first string.

Practice Point 4: Then I move up to 9th position and play another A triad. I play E at the 9th fret on the third string with my first finger, then A at the 10th fret on the second with my third finger, and then C# at the 9th fret on the first string with my second finger. I forward roll across strings 3, 2, and 1.

Practice Point 5: Now I play the same roll, but this time I'm going to add the fourth finger of my left hand on E at the 12th fret on the first string. I pick 3, 2, 1 again, but this time the notes are E, A, E.

Practice Point 6: Then I slide my left hand up to 14th position and barre across the second and third strings with my first finger. I play A on the third string, C# on the second string, and then with my fourth finger I play A at the 17th fret on the first string. I pick 3, 2, 1 again.

Combining These Exercises

Now we'll combine the first few exercises and turn them into licks in the key of G. This is something called a *tag*. A tag is something you play at the end of a tune, to kind of put your signature on it. You've heard Chet Atkins and a lot of people play this lick. It's a standard country tag over the chords G, C, and D. It's very banjo-esque, using the forward roll.

Figure 4: A Standard Country Tag

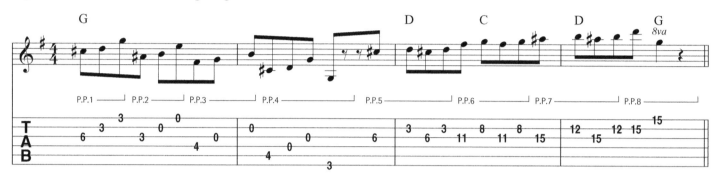

Practice Point 1: I barre across the top two strings at the 3rd fret with my first finger and play C# at the 6th fret on the third string with my fourth finger. I do a forward roll across strings 3, 2, and 1. I play C#, D, and G. So you get that minor second interval (the C# against the D at the 3rd fret on the second string), which sounds dissonant. When you get it up to tempo, it will sound like what it's supposed to sound like. Also, in order to get that sleazy country sound, I'm bending the first note of each sequence up just a little bit. So I bend the C# up with my fourth finger.

Practice Point 2: On the second roll, I play A# at the 3rd fret on the third string with my third finger, then play the second and first strings open. It's a forward roll again. I play A#, B, and E. I bend the A# a little.

Practice Point 3: Then I go down to the fourth string and put my second finger on F# with my second finger, then play the third string open and the second string open. I roll across strings 4, 3, and 2, playing F#, G, and B. I bend the F# a little.

Practice Point 4: Then I play C# at the 4th fret on the fifth string with my second finger, then strings 4 and 3 open. I play C#, D, and G. I bend the C# a little. Then I play G at the 3rd fret on the sixth string.

Practice Point 5: The rest of the tag takes place on strings 3 and 2, and it's just the notes of a G triad. I approach each note from a half step below, and from another string. I slide my fourth finger from C at the 5th fret on the third string to C# at the 6th fret. I hit that string with my pick. Then, with the middle finger of my right hand and the first finger on my left hand, I play D at the 3rd fret on the second string. I play those notes twice: C#, D, C#, D. It's an alternating motion with the pick and middle finger. Don't try to do it all with the pick because you won't get it as fast. I use this same alternating pick-middle finger motion throughout the rest of this tag.

Practice Point 6: I move up to 8th position. My fourth finger is on F# at the 11th fret on the third string, and my first finger is on G at the 8th fret on the second string. I play F#, G, F#, G.

Practice Point 7: Then I move up to 12th position. My fourth finger is on A# at the 15th fret on the third string, and my first finger is on B at the 12th fret on the second string. I play A#, B, A#, B.

Practice Point 8: Then I barre with my fourth finger at the 15th fret on the first and second strings, and play D on the second string and G on the first string.

The Solo

Now we'll take our banjo roll technique and apply it to this chapter's solo.

Phrase 1

Practice Point 1: In my left hand, I barre the top two strings at the 5th fret with my first finger. Then with my second finger, I play C♯ at the 6th fret on the third string. I pluck those three notes all together, with my pick on the third string, middle finger on the second string, and ring finger on the first string.

Practice Point 2: Then I pluck the same three strings, but on the third string I raise the note a half step; instead of C♯, I play D at the 7th fret with my third finger. Then I raise the note another half step and pluck the three strings again. This time I play D♯ at the 8th fret with my fourth finger. It's real dissonant at this point.

Practice Point 3: Now, while still holding the barre at the 5th fret on the first two strings, I replace my fourth finger with my third finger on D♯ on the third string. I hit the third string twice with my pick, and both times I hammer on from D♯ with my third finger to E at the 9th fret with my fourth finger. Then I play A at the 5th fret on the first string with my first finger. I pluck that note with my ring finger.

Practice Point 4: I do a forward banjo roll. I play E at the 9th fret on the third string with my pick, then E at the 5th fret on the second string with my middle finger, then A at the 5th fret on the first string with my ring finger.

Practice Point 5: I repeat Practice Points 3 and 4 one more time.

Practice Point 6: I repeat Practice Point 3 one more time, then end the lick differently. Instead of playing the E-E-A lick at the end, I play C♯ at the 6th fret on the third string with my second finger, then E at the 5th fret on the second string, and then A at the 5th fret on the first string with my first-finger barre. I end the phrase with A at the 7th fret on the fourth string with my third finger. I play that note with the pick.

Phrase 2

Phrase 2 is identical to the first half of Phrase 1.

Phrase 3

Now the chord changes to E. Over this chord, I play an open-string E lick. This is a great lick. I like this one.

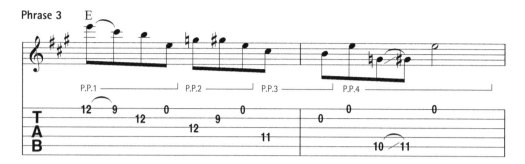

Practice Point 1: I move up to 9th position. I pull off from E at the 12th fret on the first string with my fourth finger to C# at the 9th fret with my first finger. I use the middle finger on my right hand to pluck this string once. Then I play B at the 12th fret on the second string with my fourth finger and pick. Then I play the open first string with my middle finger.

Practice Point 2: Then I play G♮ at the 12th fret on the third string with my fourth finger, G# at the 9th fret on the second string with my first finger, and open E. I play the third string with my pick, the second string with my middle finger, and the open first string with my ring finger: a forward banjo roll. So I play G♮, G#, and E.

Practice Point 3: Then I play C# at the 11th fret on the fourth string with my third finger. This time I do a forward banjo roll across strings 4, 2, and 1. I skip the third string. The second and first strings are both open. So I play C#, B, and E.

Practice Point 4: Then I slide my second finger from G♮ at the 10th fret on the fifth string to G# at the 11th fret. I pick the G♮, slide up, then play the open first string with my ring finger.

Phrase 4

This is kind of a unique lick. It sounds dissonant at a slow tempo, but it works at a faster tempo. This works over the A chord.

Practice Point 1: I play C at the 5th fret on the third string with my third finger. Then I play C# at the 2nd fret on the second string with my first finger. Then I play A at the 5th fret on the first string. I play these notes with a forward banjo roll. I play strings 3, 2, 1.

Practice Point 2: Then I play the C and C#, but I lower the top note from A to G at the 3rd fret on the first string, which I play with my second finger. Again, it's a forward banjo roll: strings 3, 2, 1.

Practice Point 3: Repeat Practice Points 1 and 2.

Phrase 5

For the D7-to-D#° lick, I use the same left hand fingering, but I slide up to the 7th position.

Practice Point 1: From C at the 5th fret, I slide up to F at the 10th fret on the third string with my third finger, F#
at the 7th fret on the second string with my first finger, and D at the 10th fret on the first string with my fourth
finger. I play these notes with a forward banjo roll. I play strings 3, 2, 1.

Practice Point 2: Then I play the F and F#, but I lower the top note from D to C at the 8th fret on the first string,
which I play with my second finger. Again, it's a forward banjo roll: strings 3, 2, 1.

Practice Point 3: Repeat Practice Points 1 and 2 without the initial slide.

Phrase 6

I wrap the solo up with a simple forward roll followed by a descending riff down the scale.

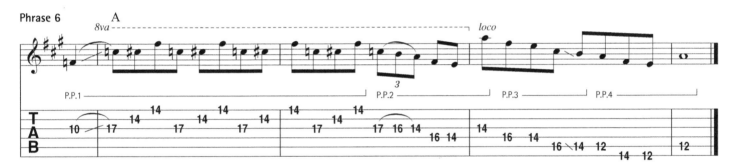

Practice Point 1: Sliding up from F at the 10th fret to C at the 17th fret with my fourth finger on the third string, I
barre the top two strings at the 14th fret with my first finger, C# and F#. I play a forward banjo roll across strings 3,
2, and 1. I play this roll four times.

Practice Point 2: Then I pull off on the third string from C at the 17th fret, to B at the 16th fret with my third
finger, to A at the 14th fret with my first finger. I hit this string once with the pick for the C note. The other two
notes are pull-offs. Then I play F# at the 16th fret on the fourth string with my third finger, E at the 14th fret with
my first finger, and go back to A at the 14th fret on the third string.

Practice Point 3: I play F# at the 16th fret on the fourth string with my third finger, and E at the 14th fret with my
first finger. Then I slide my third finger from C# at the 16th fret on the fifth string to B at the 14th fret.

Practice Point 4: Then I play A at the 12th fret on the fifth string with my first finger, F# at the 14th fret on the
sixth string with my third finger, E at the 12th fret with my first finger, and I end on A at the 12th fret on the fifth
string with my first finger.

Patience, Patience

There you have it. These banjo rolls take patience to develop, so start slow and work up your tempo gradually. Be
patient, and you'll master these rolls in no time. Work with the rhythm-only track to practice this solo, and have
fun!

2 Funky Double Stops

In this chapter, I'll explain something I call funky country double stops. This is one of my favorite styles, and I devote a lot of my practice time to it. It's become such a popular style among country guitar players that it can be heard played by almost anybody, but in particular by guys such as Albert Lee, Jerry Reed, Steve Morse, and Ray Flacke. The style goes way back, but it's been developed to the point of an art form.

I've put together a series of licks that sound like one, intact solo. But it's best to take these lick by lick. Play each one slowly, working on the right- and left-hand aspects of each one, then put it all together at the end.

Snapping Country Tone

On this recording, I used my '61 Stratocaster, set on the bridge pickup. I played through my Peavey Special 130 amp, and on my pedal board I used my compressor with a little reverb. It's a simple sound, easy to duplicate.

Also, I usually use a straight set of strings with a .010 on top. However, when I'm playing a lot of these licks where I'm constantly bending, as I do in this lesson, I find it best, for the health of my fingers, to exchange the B and G strings for a lighter gauge. So I use a .010 for the high E, .012 on B, .015 on G, .026 for D, .036 for A, and .046 for the low E. A set that goes from .010 to .046 would normally have a .013 for the B string and a .017 for the G string. Changing the B and G for lighter strings makes it a little easier to bend.

Part of the way through this lesson, your fingers are probably going to start to hurt. I've seen that many times before. If they are, just take a breather. It's going to take awhile for you to build up the necessary calluses and strength to produce these bends without bending out of tune. That is of the utmost importance when playing these licks, because it sounds terrible if you don't bend in tune. And sometimes it's a little tougher to bend in tune at tempo than it is at a slower speed. So even though you may think you have it at slow tempo, when you get it up to speed you may find that you don't quite have it down yet. So remember, have patience.

Funky Double Stops

full band   minus guitar

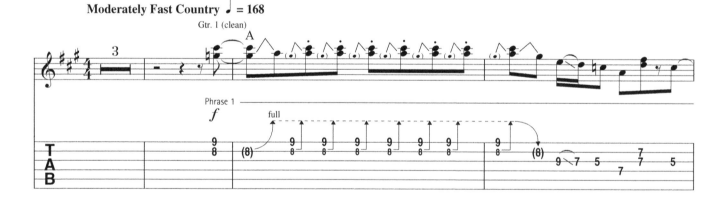

14

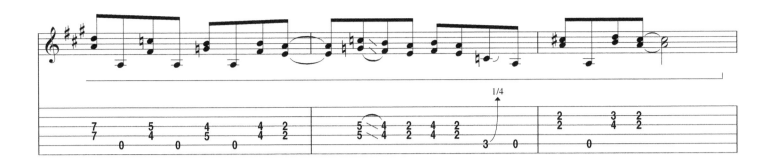

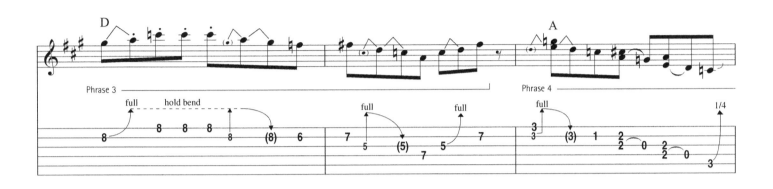

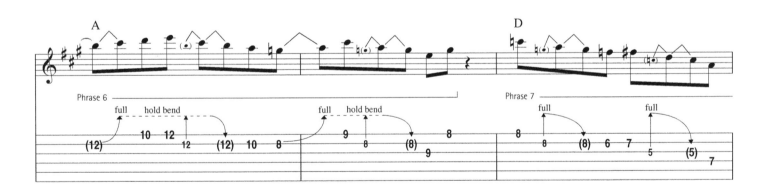

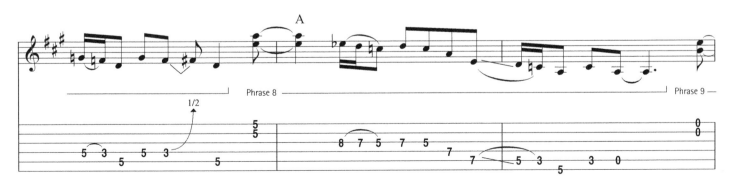

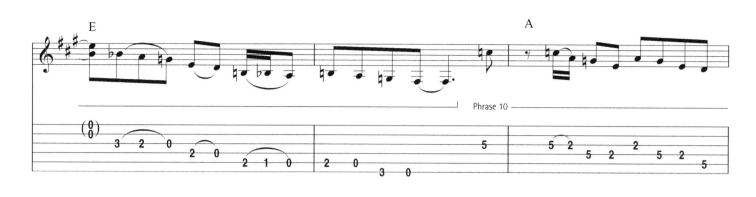

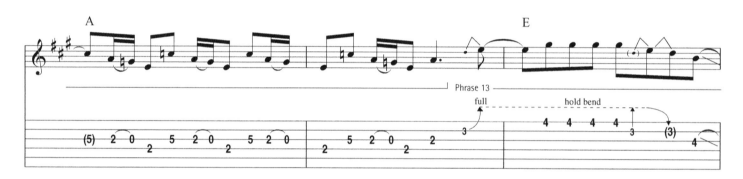

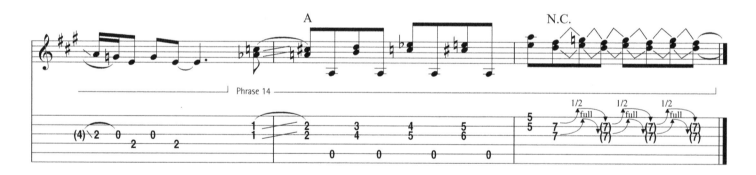

The Right Hand

I typically use my pick, middle finger, and ring finger to play this style of music. However, in order to get the snap that you hear on a lot of the licks, I sometimes tuck the pick in the palm of my hand and use my thumb, index, and middle fingers. I just pull the strings. A lot of the time, I grab the strings and just pull or pinch them between my thumb and fingers, pulling them straight up off the fingerboard and letting them snap back down. At times I don't use the pick at all. That's how I get that snap in there.

Since we're going to be alternating between pick-and-fingers, and just the fingers, I suggest that you find a comfortable place for your pick somewhere in your right hand. I tuck the pick in between the second knuckle and where my middle finger meets my palm. So I can use just my fingers, or grab my pick and use it and my fingers. So find a place in your right hand where you can tuck your pick away at a moment's notice, and grab it at a moment's notice when you need it.

The Solo

Phrase 1

Phrase 1 is the perfect example of not using the pick at all. For this particular lick, I use nothing but my thumb and index and middle fingers on my right hand.

Practice Point 1: I tuck my pick away and, with my index and middle fingers, grab the two notes on the top two strings: G at the 8th fret on the second string and C♯ at the 9th fret on the first string. I just grab the two notes and snap them—pull them straight up off the fingerboard and let them snap back like a rubber band. With my left hand, I've got my fourth finger on C♯ on the first string, and with my third finger I bend G up to A. I support the bend with my first and second fingers, placing them on the string behind the third finger and using them to help bend. For the remainder of the measure I pluck those notes in eighth notes, real staccato, with the second string bent to A and the C♯ on top.

Practice Point 2: Then I release the bend. I hit the A and C♯ together on beat one of the second measure, then, while still holding the C♯, release the A to G on the "and" of beat 1. If you try to do this lick with a pick, it doesn't come across nearly as staccato, or funky, so you want to use just the two fingers. To make it real staccato, stop each note from ringing after it has been played. I stick the fingers of my picking hand on the string and muffle it that way. This is probably one of the hardest licks in the entire solo, because you have to get your right hand going very fast.

Practice Point 3: Then I use my index finger to slide from E at the 9th fret on the third string to D at the 7th fret, and follow it with C at the 5th fret, then A at the 7th fret on the fourth string with my third finger. As far as my right hand fingering goes, I play the notes on the third string with my index finger, and the A with my thumb. I pluck really hard so I get that snap.

Practice Point 4: Then I flatten my third finger out to play a double stop with D at the 7th fret on the third string and F♯ at the 7th fret on the second string.

Practice Point 5: The rest of the lick is all single notes. I start with C at the 5th fret on the third string, and bend it a little. I use my index finger to pick this note. I play A at the 7th fret on the fourth string, G at the 5th fret. Then I play E at the 7th fret on the fifth string with my third finger, slide it down to D at the 5th fret, then play C at the 3rd fret with my first finger. Every time I hit the C—the minor third in this key—I pull it a little toward C♯.

Practice Point 6: Then I play open A, F♯ at the 2nd fret on the 6th string, A, F♯ again, then C on the fifth string, ending with the open A.

Phrase 2

For Phrase 2, I haven't even grabbed my pick yet. I play this one with just the thumb, middle, and index fingers of my right hand. A big part of this lick is the interplay between the open A bass note and the double stops. It kind of gives it a jagged, angular feeling that makes it stand out.

Practice Point 1: The lick starts in the 5th position. I place my third finger on D at the 7th fret on the third string, and my fourth finger on F♯ at the 7th fret on the second string. I bend both of those notes before I actually pluck them with my right hand. I bend them a whole step, so the D sounds like E and the F♯ sounds like G♯. I pluck them together after I've bent them up, then release them on the "and" of beat 1.

Here's a trick I've learned about bending double stops in tune: when you have to bend two notes, as in this lick, put your two fingers on the notes, then pretend that your two fingers are welded together, so you can not move one finger independently of the other. They can only move together. Then hit the two strings, and concentrate on bending your weakest finger in tune. My weakest finger is my fourth finger. I can bend from here to Seattle—I'm in Los Angeles, by the way—with my third finger, but my fourth finger is weak. So I concentrate on bending with my weakest finger. When I concentrate on bending F♯ up to G♯ and I keep the two strings parallel, somehow, as if by wizardry, the D will go up to E. The strings remain parallel. So always concentrate on bending your weakest finger in tune, and the other finger will follow.

Practice Point 2: Then I barre the 5th fret on the second and third strings, the C and E, with my first finger. Then I play A at the 7th fret on the fourth string with my third finger. Then I barre my third finger at the 7th fret on the second and third strings, the D and F♯, and then go back to A on the fourth string. Then I play a double stop with C at the 5th fret on the third string with my second finger and E♭ at the 4th fret on the second string with my first finger. On the "and" of the fourth beat, I slide that shape up one fret to play C♯ at the 6th fret on the third string and E at the 5th fret on the second string. In order to reinforce the time value of both double stops, I pick both double stops, using my index and middle finger to snap the strings.

Practice Point 3: Then I get to a part where I alternate the double stops with an open A bass line that I play with my thumb. First I play A at the 7th fret on the fourth string and D at the 7th fret on the third string with a third-finger barre, then the open A. Then I play F♯ at the 4th fret on the fourth string with my first finger and C at the 5th fret on the third string with my second finger, then open A again. Then I reverse my fingers and play G at the 5th fret on the fourth string with my second finger and B at the 4th fret on the third string with my first finger, then hit another open A.

Practice Point 4: Then I barre the 4th fret on the fourth and third strings with my third finger to play F♯ and B, then barre with my first finger at the 2nd fret to play E and A.

Practice Point 5: Then I slide with a third-finger barre from the 5th fret on the fourth and third strings to the 4th fret. I then play a first-finger barre at the 2nd fret on the fourth and third strings. Then I play the 4th-fret barre again, then back to the 2nd-fret barre.

Practice Point 6: Then I play C at the 3rd fret on the fifth string, bending it just a little, then open A. Then with my first finger, I barre the 2nd fret on the third and second strings to play A and C#, then play an open A, then end the lick by playing B at the 4th fret on the third string and D at the 3rd fret on the second string, then the A and C# again.

Phrase 3

The chord changes to D at this point, so I have to play a D lick. I use my pick on this one. Every note is played with a pick.

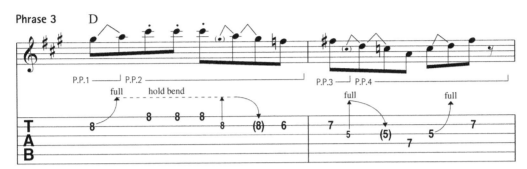

Practice Point 1: I place my third finger on G at the 8th fret on the second string, pick the note, and bend it to A. I hold this bent note throughout the first half of this lick.

Practice Point 2: Then with my fourth finger, I play C at the 8th fret on the first string and pick three times, real staccato. After the third C note, I release the bent A back to G. Then I play F at the 6th fret on the second string with my first finger.

Practice Point 3: Now I shift positions. Here's where it gets tough. I go to 5th position and put my fourth finger on F# at the 7th fret on the second string. I hit that note and actually hold it for three beats.

Practice Point 4: Meanwhile, I place my first finger on C at the 5th fret on the third string and bend it up to D. I bend before I pick the note so that when I pick it, it sounds like D. Then, while still holding the F# on the second string, I release the bent third string to play C. Then, I play A at the 7th fret on the fourth string. Then I play the C and bend it back to D. Finally, on the fourth beat, I play the F#, which I've been holding all this time anyway.

This is a first-finger bend, but it's not a standard first-finger bend in that you're not pulling the string toward the floor. You're pushing the note up toward the ceiling because the F# must ring underneath it.

Phrase 4

We go back to A for this lick. I tuck my pick away again for this one. I use all fingers on this lick, especially my index and middle fingers.

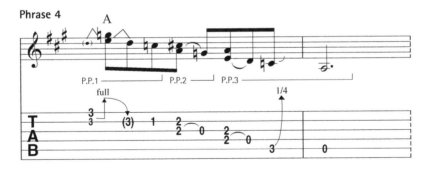

Practice Point 1: I start with my fourth finger on G at the 3rd fret on the first string. At the same time, I use my third finger to play D at the 3rd fret on the second string, bent up to E. I bend it before I actually play it, so that when I play it, it sounds like I'm playing E and G together. Then I release the bend so that the note drops to D on "and" of beat 1. Then I play C at the 1st fret on the second string with my first finger.

Practice Point 2: Now I play A at the 2nd fret on the third string with my second finger and C# at the 2nd fret on the second string with my third finger. I pluck both of them together with the index and middle fingers of my right hand, and then pull off my second finger from A and let the open G string ring with the C#.

Practice Point 3: Then I go down to strings 3 and 4 and play the same rhythm, placing my second finger on E at the 2nd fret on the fourth string and my third finger on A at the 2nd fret on the third string. I pluck both notes together, then pull off with my second finger to the open D. Then, with my fourth finger, I play C at the 3rd fret on the fifth string, bend it a little, then play the open A string. I play those last two notes with my right-hand thumb.

Phrase 5

Phrase 5 is played over an E chord. I play this one with my pick, middle, and ring fingers. This takes place in 9th position, and I play primarily on the second, third, and fourth strings.

Practice Point 1: I barre the 9th fret on the second, third, and fourth strings with my first finger. I play all the notes on the fourth string with my pick, all the notes on the third string with the middle finger of my right hand, and all the notes on the second string with my ring finger. I play E on the third string and G# on the second string with my fingers, then play B on the fourth string with my pick.

Practice Point 2: Then I play F# at the 11th fret on the third string with my third finger, and A at the 10th fret on the second string with my second finger. I use the middle and ring fingers on my right hand to pluck those strings. I slide that shape up one fret, then up another fret. So this lick is parallel thirds. Then I flatten my second finger out at the 12th fret on the first and second strings to play B and E. Again, I pluck those notes with my middle and ring fingers.

Practice Point 3: Then I go back down to the shape I played in Practice Point 2. I play G at the 12th fret on the third string with my third finger and Bb at the 11th fret on the second string with my second finger. I quickly slide that shape down one fret to pluck F# and A, then hit B at the 9th fret on the fourth string with my first finger and pick. I repeat this move.

Practice Point 4: I end the phrase with F# and A again. Then, with my first finger, I barre at the 9th fret on the second and third strings and play E and G#.

Phrase 6

Phrase 6 takes place in 10th position on the first and second strings. It's kind of similar to Phrase 3. I play this phrase with my pick, and not my fingers.

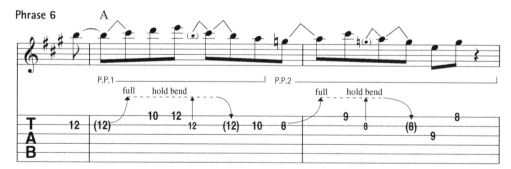

Practice Point 1: I start by bending B at the 12th fret on the second string to C# with my third finger. Underneath that on the first string, while letting the C# ring, I play D at the 10th fret with my first finger, then E at the 12th fret with my fourth finger. Then I release the bend to B, then play A at the 10th fret on the second string with my first finger.

Practice Point 2: Then I shift down to 7th position. I bend G at the 8th fret on the second string to A with my second finger. I hold that note and play C# at the 9th fret on the first string with my fourth finger. Then I release the bend back to G. Then I play E at the 9th fret on the third string with my third finger, and then G again.

Phrase 7

Now we go back to the D chord. This is kind of a variation on Phrase 3. We're going to do the same series of bends, but change the rhythm a little bit. I play this phrase with my pick, too.

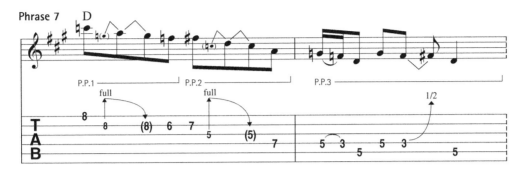

Practice Point 1: I start with C at the 8th fret on the first string with my fourth finger. Then while holding that note, I bend G at the 8th fret on the second string up to A with my third finger. I bend the note to A before I play it, so it sounds like A when I play it. Then I release that note back to G, then play F at the 6th fret with my first finger.

Practice Point 2: Then I move to 5th position and play F♯ at the 7th fret on the second string with my fourth finger. Then, while holding the F♯, I bend C at the 5th fret on the third string up to D, then release back to C. I push the string up toward the ceiling with my first finger. Then I play A at the 7th fret on the fourth string with my third finger.

Practice Point 3: Then I slide my third finger down to G at the 5th fret, pull off to F at the 3rd fret, then play D at the 5th fret on the fifth string with my third finger. Then I flatten my third finger into a barre and play G on the fourth string again. Then I play F on the fourth string with my first finger and bend it very deliberately up to F♯. I want it to take the time value of two eighth notes. Then I play D on the fifth string again.

Phrase 8

This phrase, in A, is a standard rock lick. It's fairly easy to play.

Practice Point 1: I barre at the 5th fret on the first and second strings. I play those notes, E and A, then pull off from E♭ to D to C on the third string. I play E♭ at the 8th fret with my third finger, pull off to D at the 7th fret, then pull off to C at the 5th fret. I do this all with my pick. Then I play D, C, and A at the 7th fret on the fourth string with my third finger.

Practice Point 2: Then I shift my third finger over to the fifth string. I play E at the 7th fret, then slide down to D at the 5th fret, play C at the 3rd fret with my first finger, then play A at the 5th fret on the sixth string with my third finger. Then I play C again and then the open A string. So the first A is on the sixth string, the second A is the open fifth string.

Phrase 9

This is another standard rock lick, similar to Phrase 8. This one is over the E chord, and it's played in the open position.

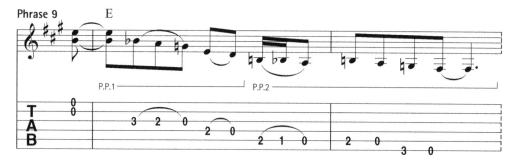

Practice Point 1: I start with the top two strings open. Then I pull off from B♭ at the 3rd fret on the third string with my third finger, to A at the 2nd fret with my second finger, to the open G string. Then I play E at the 2nd fret on the fourth string with my second finger and pull off to the open D string.

Practice Point 2: Then I go down to the fifth string and pull off from B at the 2nd fret with my second finger, to B♭ at the 1st fret with my first finger, to open A. Then I play B♮, open A, G at the 3rd fret on the sixth string with my third finger, then open E.

Phrase 10

This phrase is over an A chord. It's single notes, with the pick.

Practice Point 1: I play C at the 5th fret on the third string with my fourth finger. Then I hit it again and pull off to A at the 2nd fret with my first finger. Then I play G at the 5th fret on the fourth string with my fourth finger, then E at the 2nd fret with my first finger.

Practice Point 2: Then I go back to A, then back down to G, E, and then D at the 5th fret on the fifth string with my fourth finger.

Practice Point 3: Then I play C at the 3rd fret on the fifth string with my second finger, then open A. Then I jump back up an octave and play C to A on the third string again.

Phrase 11

This phrase is very similar to Phrase 10. It's a repeating sequence. I play this phrase over the D chord.

Practice Point 1: I start with the C at the 5th fret on the third string again, then hit A at the 2nd fret, then pull off to open G. Then I play E at the 2nd fret on the fourth string with my first finger. I repeat this lick four times, then hit B at the 4th fret on the third string with my third finger. I bend that B up a little bit, about a quarter step or so.

Phrase 12

This phrase is nearly identical to Phrase 11 and is played over the A chord. The timing of this phrase and Phrase 11 is very important. They're both quick licks, and they have to fit right into the timing of the groove.

Practice Point 1: Identical to Phrase 11, Practice Point 1, except that I end with my first finger on A at the 2nd fret on the third string, instead of the B that ended Phrase 11. I don't bend the A note.

Phrase 13

This phrase is played over the E chord. I tuck my pick away and use my fingers on this phrase. You can hear it snap.

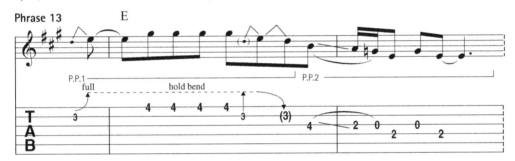

Practice Point 1: I start in 3rd position. I bend D at the 3rd fret on the second string up to E with my first finger. I bend the note as soon as I pick it, then hold it while I play G♯ at the 4th fret on the first string with my third finger. I play the G♯ four times. Then I release the bend to D.

Practice Point 2: Then I play B at the 4th fret on the second string with my second finger. I slide down to A at the 2nd fret, then pull off to the open G string. Then I play E at the 2nd fret on the fourth string, the open G again, and end the phrase on E on the fourth string.

Phrase 14

This phrase wraps up the tune with some really cool double stops. I use my pick and fingers on this phrase.

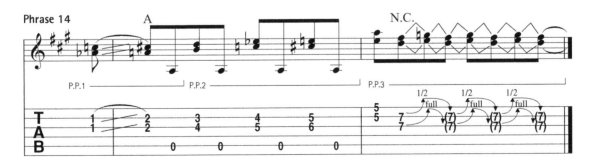

Practice Point 1: I start with a slide. I use my first finger to barre the second and third strings at the 1st fret and immediately slide it up to the 2nd fret to play A and C♯. Then I hit an open A string with the pick.

Practice Point 2: Then I play B at the 4th fret on the third string with my third finger and D at the 3rd fret on the second string with my second finger together. I hit the open A, then slide the double stop up one fret to play C and E♭, hit the open A again, then slide the double stop up one more fret to play C♯ and E, followed again by the open A.

Practice Point 3: Then I barre the 5th fret on the top two strings with my first finger, play those notes, then place my third finger on D at the 7th fret on the third string and my fourth finger on F♯ at the 7th fret on the second string. I bend those notes up, release, bend up again, release again. I do this several times, like a wide, double-stop vibrato at the tempo of the tune.

Congratulations

Now we've finished studying and taking all these phrases. Work on them slowly, and gradually work up the tempo. Don't forget to give your hands a rest if necessary, and remember to be patient. The skills necessary to bend these double stops in tune takes time to develop.

3 Pedal-Steel Mania

In this chapter, I'm going to show you how to simulate the pedal steel guitar. There are a couple of things to keep in mind about pedal steel before we jump into this lesson. To simulate the tone of a pedal steel, you'll want to use as much treble as you can get. Use your bridge pickup. Also, when I'm trying to get the pedal-steel tone, I turn the treble on my amplifier up a couple of notches higher than I normally would. I also turn the reverb up a little higher than I normally would to give it a little more sustain. Pedal steel guitars have more sustain than normal guitars, so that's the way we make up for it.

Also, I use lighter B and G strings on my guitar to make it easier to bend on those strings. The gauges I use on the Strat I recorded this lesson with are .010, .012, .015, .026, .036, .046. Most of the bending takes place on the B and G strings, and there's no sense in hurting yourself. So put on a lighter B and G string and make it easier.

Pedal-Steel Mania

full band minus guitar

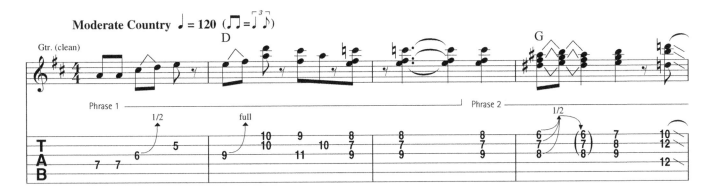

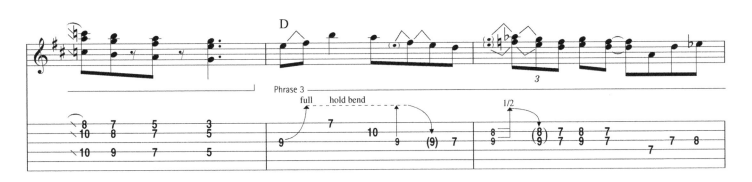

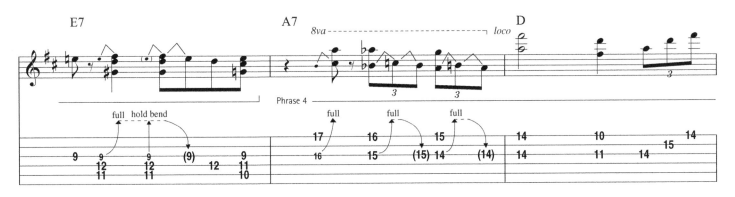

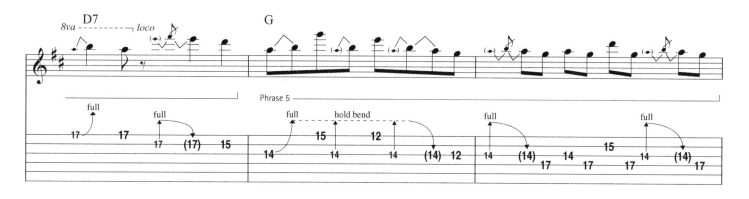

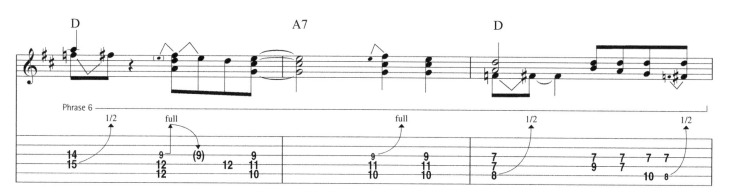

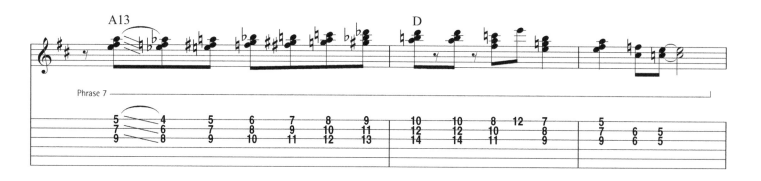

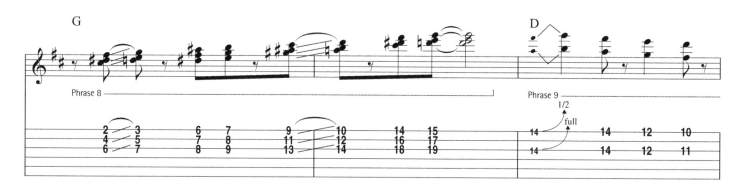

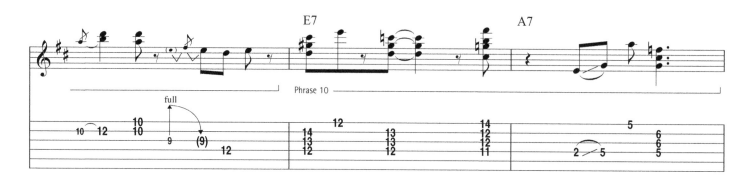

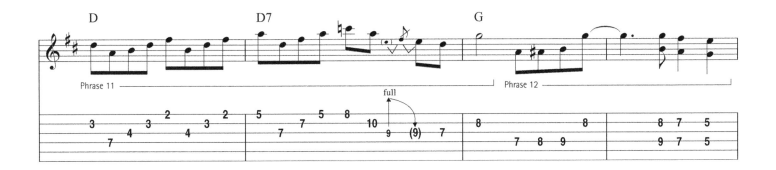

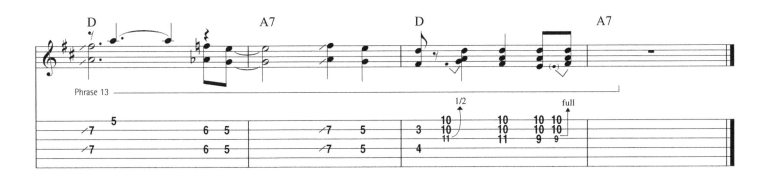

The Solo

Phrase 1

This solo starts with a simple pickup beginning on beat 2, then it goes to a couple of great sounding chord shapes.

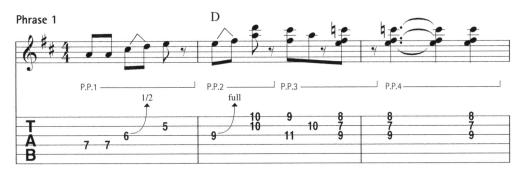

Practice Point 1: This lick takes place in 5th position. I start on A at the 7th fret on the fourth string, play that note twice with my third finger, then reach for C# at the 6th fret on the third string with my second finger. I hit the C#, then bend it up to D. Then I play E at the 5th fret on the second string with my first finger. I pick all these notes.

Practice Point 2: Now I shift up to play E at the 9th fret on the third string with my third finger. I hit that E note and bend it up to F#, then lay my fourth finger down as a barre across the top two strings at the 10th fret, playing A and D together. I hold the bent F# while I play the A and D.

Practice Point 3: Then I play a D major seventh triad in 9th position. I fret F# at the 11th fret on the third string with my third finger, A at the 10th fret on the second string with my second finger, and C# at the 9th fret on the first string with my first finger. I play the F# and C# together, using my pick on the F# and the ring finger on my right hand on the C#. Then my middle finger plays the A.

Practice Point 4: Then I shift down to 7th position and get a real pedal-steel chord voicing. I play E at the 9th fret on the third string with my third finger, F# at the 7th fret on the second string with my first finger, and C♮ at the 8th fret on the first string with my second finger. I pluck all three notes together, with the pick on E, my middle finger on F#, and my ring finger on C. It's a nice voicing. I pluck the chord twice.

Phrase 2

This phrase includes a cool three-string bend that actually isn't too difficult, and some great octave/sixth phrasings that outline a G scale.

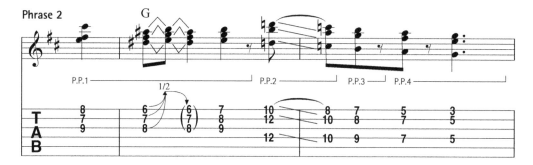

Practice Point 1: I play the final chord from Phrase 1 one time, then bend into a G6 chord. The G6 chord consists of E at the 9th fret on the third string, which I play with my third finger; G at the 8th fret on the second string, which I play with my second finger; and B at the 7th fret on the first string, which I play with my first finger. I actually start with this same chord shape one fret lower and bend all three strings up a half step, or one fret, to play G6. Then I release the bend, then actually slide up a fret and pluck the G6 chord. Again, I use the pick and my middle and ring fingers to pluck this chord.

Practice Point 2: Then I go up to 10th position. I play D at the 12th fret on the fourth string with my third finger, B at the 12th fret on the second string with my fourth finger, and D at the 10th fret on the first string with my first finger; it's just an octave with a sixth in the middle. I pluck these three notes with my pick, middle, and ring fingers. Then I slide that same shape down two frets.

Practice Point 3: After playing the C octave/sixth shape, I slide the octaves down one fret to play B at the 9th fret on the fourth string and at the 7th fret on the first string, and with my second finger I play G at the 8th fret on the second string. So this note is one fret lower than it was on the D and C octaves. Again, I pluck all three notes together.

Practice Point 4: Then I go back to the shape I used on D and C in Practice Point 2, to play A at the 7th fret on the fourth string, and G at the 5th fret on the fourth string.

Phrase 3

This is the toughest lick in the whole solo. It took me a long time to get it right, because I had to do some first-finger bends. But work it out one step at a time, and you'll get it.

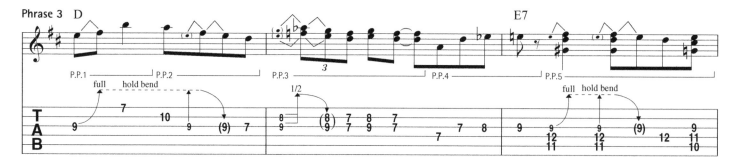

Practice Point 1: This phrase starts in 7th position. I play E at the 9th fret on the third string with my third finger and bend it a whole step to F♯. Then I play B at the 7th fret on the first string with my first finger. I hold the bent F♯ while I play B.

Practice Point 2: Then, while still holding the F♯, and still letting the B ring as well, I play A at the 10th fret on the second string with my fourth finger. Then I pick the F♯ again and release the bend to E. I resolve that to D at the 7th fret on the third string with my first finger.

Practice Point 3: Now I play double stops. I fret E at the 9th fret on the third string with my third finger and G at the 8th fret on the second string with my second finger. I bend both notes up a half step before I pick them, so I actually play F and A♭. Then I release the bend. Then I play a first-finger barre at the 7th fret on the second and third strings, so I play D and F♯. Then I play the E and G and again, and then the D and F♯ again.

The bend is really important because we have to sound like we're playing with a bar, the bar the pedal steel players use. They slide that bar along the strings to get that sound. We can't get that sound, so we have to imitate it by bending double stops.

Practice Point 4: I play A at the 7th fret on the fourth string with my first finger, then D at the 7th fret on the third string with my first finger, then E♭ at the 8th fret with my second finger, then E at the 9th fret with my third finger.

Practice Point 5: Now comes the tough part: the first-finger bend. I play an E7 chord with G♯ at the 11th fret on the fifth string with my third finger, D at the 12th fret on the fourth string with my fourth finger, and E at the 9th fret on the third string with my first finger. I pluck all three notes together, then, while holding the chord, bend the third string with my first finger up to F♯. I actually bend the string toward the floor. Then I pluck the chord again and release the bend to E. Then I play D on the fourth string by itself, while letting the chord ring.

Then I slide my third and fourth finger down one fret, so that my third finger is on G♮ at the 10th fret on the fifth string and my fourth finger is on C♯ at the 11th fret on the fourth string. At the same time, I play E at the 9th fret on the third string with my first finger, and I pluck all three notes together. So this chord sounds like a strong resolve from the chord before. This is a classic pedal-steel move.

Be Sure To Bend In Tune

Occasionally you'll notice that you're not bending in tune. That's one of the hardest things about simulating a pedal steel guitar on a regular six-string guitar. You have to be really precise in your bends. You have to bend to the exact note that you want to bend to. You can't bend to somewhere in the vicinity. You can get away with that playing rock and blues, but when you play country, your bending technique has to be very precise. So these bends are going to require some practice.

Phrase 4

This phrase consists of some simple chromatic moves over the A7 rhythm, then outlines the D chord.

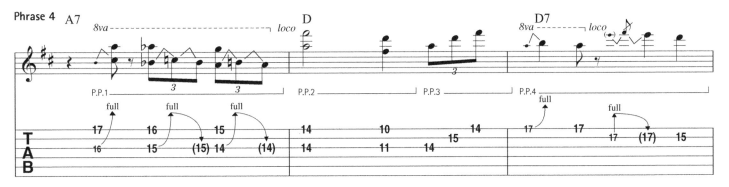

Practice Point 1: I play A at the 17th fret on the first string with my fourth finger and B at the 16th fret on the third string with my third finger. I pluck both strings together, bending B up a whole step to C♯ as soon as I hit the notes. Then I move that same shape down one fret, doing the same bend on third string, but releasing the bend too. So on that move, I play A♭ at the 16th fret on the first string with my fourth finger and B♭ at the 15th fret on the third string with my third finger. I pluck the two notes, bend B♭ to C, then release it to B♭ again, letting it ring the whole time. Then I move down one more fret and do that move again, including the bend and release on the third string.

Practice Point 2: I play A at the 14th fret on the third string with my third finger, together with F♯ at the 14th fret on the first string with my fourth finger. Then I drop down to 10th position and play F♯ at the 11th fret on the third string with my second finger and D at the 10th fret with my first finger.

Practice Point 3: Then I go back up to the 14th fret and play a D triad arpeggio. I barre the 14th fret across the top three strings with my first finger and play A at the 14th fret on the third string with my first finger, D at the 15th fret on the second string with my second finger, and F♯ at the 14th fret on the first string with my first finger.

Practice Point 4: Then I play A at the 17th fret on the first string with my fourth finger, bend it immediately up a whole step to B, then release it back to A. Then I pre-bend E at the 17th fret on the second string up a whole step to F♯ with my fourth finger. A pre-bend is when you bend the note before you pick it, so that all you hear is the already bent note. Usually you pre-bend so that you can pick the higher note and release it to the unbent note. I resolve the bent F♯ to E, then play D at the 15th fret with my second finger.

Phrase 5

Phrase 5 outlines the G chord in 12th position.

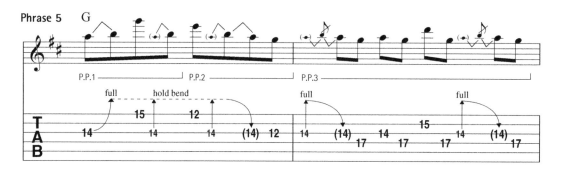

Practice Point 1: I play A at the 14th fret on the third string with my third finger and bend it up a whole step to B. Then while holding the bend, I play G at the 15th fret on the first string with my fourth finger. Then I play the bent B again.

Practice Point 2: Then I play E at the 12th fret on the first string with my first finger. Then I pick the bent B again, release it to A, then play G at the 12th fret on the third string with my first finger.

Practice Point 3: This is a neat lick. I fret A at the 14th fret on the third string with my first finger. Then I fret G at the 17th fret on the fourth string with my fourth finger. With my second finger, I fret D at the 15th fret on the second string with my second finger. I pre-bend the A to B, hit that note, then release it to A. Then I play G on the fourth string, while still holding the A. I quickly play the G, then A again. Then I play the D on the second string, G on the fourth string, then do the pre-bend again, picking the bent B, releasing it to A, then playing G on the fourth string again.

Phrase 6

Phrase 6 includes some lush sounding chords, and a couple of tricky first-finger bends.

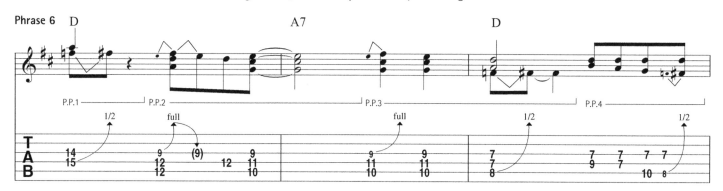

Practice Point 1: I keep my first finger on A, right where it was in Phrase 5. I play that note and at the same time I play F at the 15th fret on the fourth string with my second finger, bending it up a half step to F♯.

Practice Point 2: This is another lick with a first-finger bend. I play A at the 12th fret on the fifth string with my third finger, D at the 12th fret on the fourth string with my fourth finger, and I fret E at the 9th fret on the third string with my first finger. I bend the E up a whole step to F♯, then I release it to E, play the D by itself, and then play an A7 chord. I keep my first finger on E for the A7 chord, and play G at the 10th fret on the fifth string with my second finger and C♯ at the 11th fret on the fourth string with my fourth finger.

Practice Point 3: I pluck the A7 chord again, then bend the E a whole step up to F♯, then release it again. Then I resolve to a D chord in 7th position. I play F♮ at the 8th fret on the fifth string with my second finger and barre with my first finger at the 7th fret across the fourth and third strings. I pluck those three notes—F, A, and D—together, then bend the F to F♯.

Practice Point 4: Then, while holding the A and D with the first-finger barre at the 7th fret on the fourth and third strings, I place my third finger on B at the 9th fret on the fourth string and play B and D together, then I play A and D together. Then I play the D together with G at the 10th fret on the fifth string, which I play with my fourth finger. When I reach for the G, I still let both the A and D on the fourth and third strings ring, and I let them keep ringing through the end of the lick. I end the phrase with D and F♯. I actually play F at the 8th fret on the fifth string with my second finger and bend it up to F♯. I pluck all these double stops with my pick and middle finger.

Phrase 7

I start the second chorus with one of my favorite pedal-steel licks. It's a chromatic phrase using 6th or 13th chords. The first chorus was more traditional, using more of a 9th chord tonality. In this chorus, we get a little jazzier. You'll recognize it right away when you hear the difference in the chords.

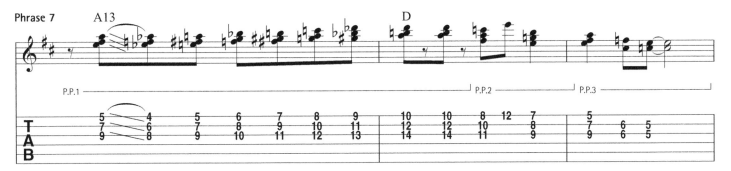

Practice Point 1: The first run isn't too hard, though the stretch might be a little tough at first. I play E at the 9th fret on the third string with my fourth finger, F♯ at the 7th fret on the second string with my second finger, and A at the 5th fret on the first string with my first finger. This is a very close-voiced D9 chord, with the 3rd (F♯), the 5th (A), and the 9th (E) of the chord. I pluck the chord, slide it back one fret without plucking it, then slide it back and pluck it again. Then I take that same chord shape and slide it up chromatically, one fret at a time, plucking each time, until I'm playing with my first finger on D at the 10th fret on the first string. I pluck the three strings together with my pick, middle, and ring fingers. You don't want to strum these; you want to pluck them so all the notes sound at the same time and you get the pedal-steel sound.

Practice Point 2: Now I move down to a D7 voicing. I play F♯ at the 11th fret on the third string with my third finger, A at the 10th fret on the second string with my second finger, and C at the 8th fret on the first string with my first finger. I strum the chord with a downstroke, then play E at the 12th fret on the first string with my fourth finger. Then I move down and play an E minor triad in 7th position. I play E at the 9th fret on the third string with my third finger, G at the 8th fret on the second string with my second finger, and B at the 7th fret on the first string with my first finger.

Practice Point 3: Then I play the original chord shape as described in Practice Point 1, with the E, F♯, and A. Then I barre with my first finger at the 6th fret across the second and third strings and play C♯ and F♮. And finally I slide that down one fret to play C♮ and E at the 5th fret.

Phrase 8

This phrase involves more close-voiced chords. Close-voiced means that most of the notes in the chord are within a one-octave range of each other. In Phrase 7, the notes were E, F♯, and A, all within a 4th of each other. In Phrase 8, I use the same chord shape, starting a little lower on the neck. The notes are D, E, and G—again, three chord tones bunched together within a 4th, from the lowest to the highest note. In this case, however, the chord is functioning as a G6 chord, with the 5th (D), the 6th (E), and the root (G).

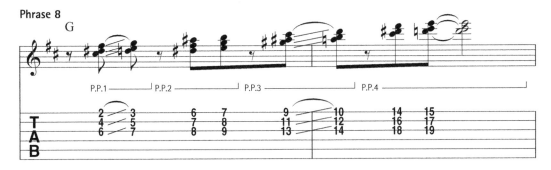

31

Practice Point 1: I start by sliding into the G6 chord from a half step below. To finger the G6, I play D at the 7th fret on the third string with my fourth finger, E at the 5th fret on the second string with my second finger, and G at the 3rd fret on the first string with my first finger. I play that same chord shape one fret lower, then slide up one fret and play it again.

Practice Point 2: Then I slide into an E minor triad. To play E minor, I play E at the 9th fret on the third string with my third finger, G at the 8th fret on the second string with my second finger, and B at the 7th fret on the first string with my first finger. Again, I play that same chord shape one fret lower, then slide up one fret and play it again. I don't pluck this as we did before, I just use the pick to strum down. I kind of like the sound of it.

Practice Point 3: Then I go back to the first chord shape as in Practice Point 1. This time, I play A at the 14th fret on the third string with my fourth finger, B at the 12th fret on the second string with my second finger, and D at the 10th fret on the first string with my first finger. I start one fret below and slide into this chord as well. This would function as a G9 chord, with the 9th of the chord (A), the 3rd (B), and the 5th (D). As you can see, the name given to a chord can change depending on its function with regard to the rhythm section, and a grouping of three or more notes can often be referred to by different chord names. This chord could be referred to as a D6 chord, but at this point in the song the rhythm section is playing a G chord, so it makes more sense to refer to this chord as a G9.

Practice Point 4: Identical to the move in Practice Point 1 played one fret higher.

Phrase 9

Phrase 9 uses 6th intervals, a very popular country technique. To get the pedal-steel flavor, however, I do a double-stop bend, which is a little tricky.

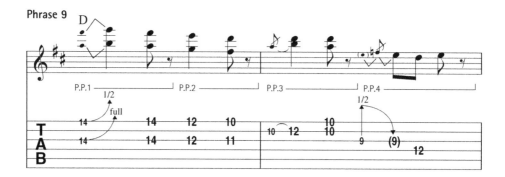

Practice Point 1: I start with A at the 14th fret on the third string with my third finger and F♯ at the 14th fret on the first string with my fourth finger. I pluck both notes together, then bend them both, the A up a whole step to B, and the F♯ up a half step to G. The trick to that is to imagine that your fingers are welded together, and they can't move independently. Put them down on the notes, then concentrate on bending your weakest finger in tune. In most cases that will be your fourth finger; it certainly is in my case. I try to keep the strings parallel. I'm not going to consciously try to bend one up a whole step and one up a half step. I concentrate on bending F# up to G with my fourth finger, and if I bend the two strings equally and keep them parallel, somehow, as if by wizardry, that A is going to go up a whole step to B. That takes some practice, but it's very effective. I play the notes, bend them up, then play them unbent again.

Practice Point 2: Then I use descending 6ths and go down to G at the 12th fret on the third string with my third finger and E at the 12th fret on the first string with my fourth finger. Then I play F♯ at the 11th fret on the third string with my second finger and D at the 10th fret on the first string with my first finger. On all these 6ths licks, I use my pick on the third string and my middle finger to pick the first string, skipping the second string entirely.

Practice Point 3: I barre with my first finger at the 10th fret across the top two strings, to play A on the second string and D on the first string. I hammer on B at the 12th fret on the second string with my third finger, then play it again without the hammer-on.

Practice Point 4: Then I play a lick we played earlier in G, this time in D. I put my first finger on E at the 9th fret on the third string. At the same time, I hold D at the 12th fret on the fourth string with my fourth finger. I start the lick with a pre-bend. I bend E on the third string up a half step to F♮, then pick the string, sounding the F, then release the bend, resolving the note to E. Then I play D on the fourth string, while still letting the E ring. Then I hit the E again.

Phrase 10

Phrase 10 is classic pedal-steel chording. I play this lick over an E7 chord, then resolve to an A7 chord.

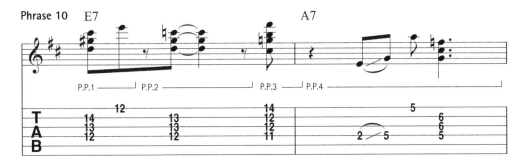

Practice Point 1: I barre with my first finger at the 12th fret across the top four strings. I add a G# at the 13th fret on the third string with my second finger, and a C# at the 14th fret on the second string with my third finger. I pluck the fourth, third, and second strings together. This is an E13 chord. Then I play the high E, which I have barred with my first finger at the 12th fret on the first string.

Practice Point 2: Now I play the same basic chord, but this time I lower the C# to C♮ at the 13th fret on the second string. I still use my third finger for this note. This is an E augmented chord.

Practice Point 3: Then I play an A13 chord in 11th position. This is a four-note chord. I play C# at the 11th fret on the fourth string with my first finger, G at the 12th fret on the third string and B at the 12th fret on the second string with a second-finger barre, and F# at the 14th fret on the first string with my fourth finger. I pluck all these notes together; I don't strum this chord. I play the fourth string with my pick, the third string with my middle finger, the second string with my ring finger, and the first string with my little finger. You want to strike all four notes at the same time to give them a real even sound.

Practice Point 4: Now I play an A augmented chord. I slide into it with my first finger from E at the 2nd fret on the fourth string to G at the 5th fret. I hold onto this note because I use it later in the measure. Then I play A at the 5th fret on the first string with my second finger. Then I pluck that G on the fourth string together with C# at the 6th fret on the third string with my third finger, and E# (F) at the 6th fret on the second string with my fourth finger. That's an A augmented chord.

Phrase 11

This is a very pedal-steel sounding, scale-based phrase. Pedal steel players play on consecutive strings, rather than playing consecutive scale tones all on one string.

Practice Point 1: The way I get A, B, and D to ring all at the same time is to stretch a little bit. I play D at the 3rd fret on the second string with my first finger. Then I play B at the 4th fret on the third string with my second finger. And I play A at the 7th fret on the fourth string with my fourth finger. I use the pick on all these notes. I play the D, then kind of sweep with a downstroke to play the A, B, then D again. Let all the strings ring together; that's how to get the steel sound.

Practice Point 2: Now I play a B minor triad on the top three strings. I play F# at the 2nd fret on the first string with my first finger, then B at the 4th fret on the third string with my third finger, then D at the 3rd fret on the second string with my second finger, then F# again. Again, sweep pick these, meaning to play the B, D, F# with downstrokes.

Practice Point 3: Then I play a D triad in 5th position. I play A at the 5th fret on the first string with my first finger. Then I play D at the 7th fret on the third string with my third finger, then F# at the 7th fret on the second string with my fourth finger, then A again. Sweep pick these, too.

Practice Point 4: Then I take that chord shape, lift off my third finger, slide my first and fourth finger up three frets to play C at the 8th fret on the first string with my first finger and A at the 10th fret on the second string with my fourth finger. Then I bend E at the 9th fret on the third string up a whole step to F# with my second finger. I pre-bend the note, so I don't pick it until it's bent. Then I release that to E. I hold the A and C up to this point, then let go of the C to play D at the 7th fret with my first finger. Then I play G at the 8th fret on the second string with my second finger.

Phrase 12

This is a simple riff featuring double-stop, descending 6ths, a very typical pedal steel-type move.

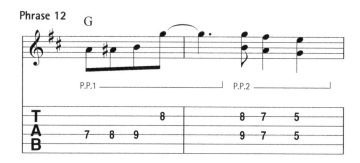

Practice Point 1: I play A at the 7th fret on the fourth string with my first finger, then A# at the 8th fret with my second finger, then B at the 9th fret with my third finger. Hold onto this B and let it ring with the next note, G at the 8th fret on the second string, which I play with my second finger.

Practice Point 2: After repeating the previous B–G double stop, I then slide down to play A at the 7th fret on the fourth string with my third finger and F# at the 7th fret on the second string with my fourth finger. I play those notes together, picking the A and plucking the F# with my ring finger. Then I slide that shape down two more frets to play G and E the 5th fret.

Phrase 13

Phrase 13 continues where Phrase 12 left off.

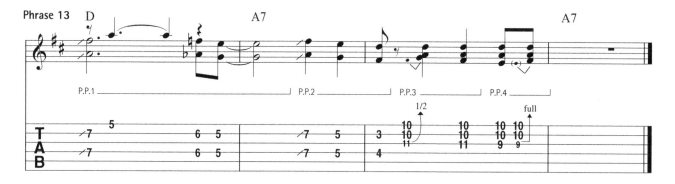

Practice Point 1: I slide the last 6th shape from Phrase 12, Practice Point 2, back up two frets to play A at the 7th fret on the fourth string and F# at the 7th fret on the second string. I pluck those two notes, then play A at the 5th fret on the first string with my first finger. I keep my third and fourth finger down on the fourth and second strings, respectively, then slide them down one fret to play Ab at the 6th fret on the fourth string and F at the 6th fret on the second string. I quickly slide that down another fret to play G and E at the 5th fret.

Practice Point 2: Then I play A and F# at the 7th fret, G and E at the 5th fret, and finally F# at the 4th fret on the fourth string with my third finger and D at the 3rd fret on the second string with my second finger. These are parallel 6th intervals.

Practice Point 3: Then I barre with my first finger at the 10th fret across the top two strings, A and D. At the same time, I fret F♯ at the 11th fret on the third string with my second finger. I bend F♯ up a half step to G, then pluck the three strings together. Then I release the bend to F♯, so I resolve a D suspended chord to a D major chord.

Practice Point 4: Then I shift down to barre the A and D at the 10th fret on the top two strings with my fourth finger. At the same time, I fret E at the 9th fret on the third string with my third finger. I pluck those three notes together, then bend the E up a whole step to F♯. And that's the end of the phrase and the solo.

4 Open-String Licks

The solo in this chapter is entitled "Open-String Licks," but I also call it the "Whiskey Jug Rag." You'll recognize this sound as one you've heard on dozens of records by Chet Atkins, Jerry Reed, Mark O'Connor, Dan Crary, and Albert Lee. It's a fairly standard technique. I'll break down this style and show you exactly what goes on.

There are two sections to the "Whiskey Jug Rag," an A and a B section. Each demonstrates a different aspect of this technique.

Open-String Tone

I played this lesson on a Fender Telecaster with EMG pickups. The Tele has a maple fingerboard, which I've had flattened a little bit to a 10-inch radius, as opposed to a 7- or 8-inch radius, which are standard Fender specs. That doesn't make any difference; it's just my personal preference. I recorded this music with a small Boss digital delay pedal and a compressor. I also double-tracked the recording, which fattens up the sound a little.

Open-String Licks

full band minus guitar

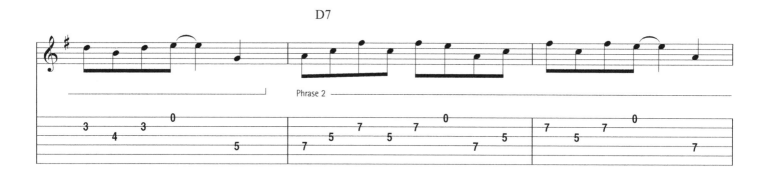

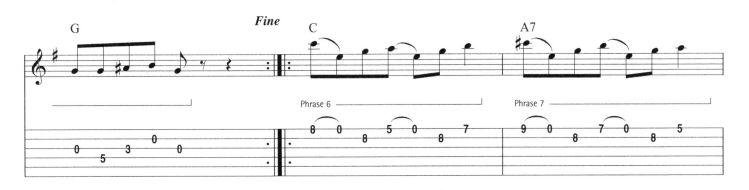

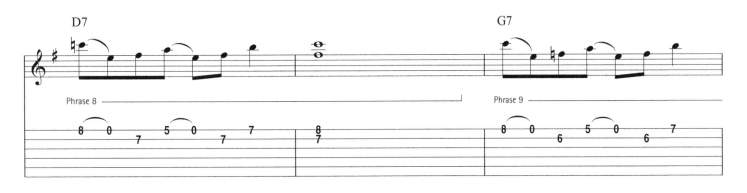

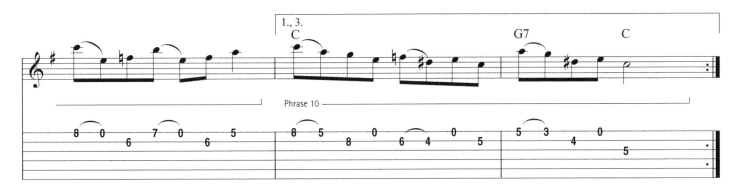

The Chord Progression

As I mentioned above, the "Whiskey Jug Rag" consists of an A and a B section. The A section starts with D7 for two measures, then G for two measures, D7 for another two, and G for just one more beat, followed by a rest for the remaining three beats of that measure and all of the eighth measure. Then play D7 for two measures, G for two measures, then E for one measure, A minor for one measure, D7 for one measure, and G for one measure. It's a 16-measure pattern, and the entire section repeats one time.

The B section of the song will also repeat after the first run through. The B section consists of C for one measure, A7 for one measure, D7 for two measures, G7 for two measures, C for one measure, then G7 for two beats and C for two beats on the first ending. The second time through the B section, you'll skip the measure that includes G7 and C. Instead, you'll just play the 2nd ending, which calls for a C chord for all four beats. Then the entire B section repeats, with both endings.

At the end of the chart, after the 2nd ending of the B section, you'll see "D.C. al Fine." That means to go back to the beginning of the song and play all the way through to the "Fine" indication. In this case, that means go back to the top of the song and play the entire A section again, two times through.

The Right Hand

For the A section of this tune, I use what I call a forward banjo roll. I use a pick, my middle finger, and the ring finger of my right hand on three consecutive strings. I use my pick on the lowest string, my middle finger on the middle string, and my ring finger on the highest string. I just forward roll. I play pick, middle finger, ring finger, in a forward roll motion. I use that forward roll technique on the A portion of this tune. You might play this technique with a thumb pick and your index and middle finger. That is perfectly acceptable. It's just not the way I do it, but either way will work.

In order to get the crisp sound that I need here, I keep the nails on my right hand about a sixteenth of an inch long, so that when I hit the string I get control by using the fleshy part of my finger, and I get the snap by pulling my finger off the string. It runs past my fingernail and bounces off my fingernail, so I kind of get that snap. You want that to happen because otherwise you're going to get the pick sound, and then you're going to get two thumps. And you don't want that. You want each note to be as crisp as every other note. So keep your fingernails just a little bit longer. Also, I put clear polish on my nails. It keeps them from breaking.

How to Approach This Style

I set up a one- or two-bar rhythmic phrase. Then against that rhythmic phrase, I use an open string that's common to all the chords in the progression. Those are the two most important aspects of what I'm doing here.

Then, as the chords change, I move triads around underneath the open string to capture the sound of the chords. Triads are any combination of three notes. For instance, for a D7 triad, I can use any three of the following notes: D, F#, A, or C. So for Phrase 1 below, I chose F#, A, and C. It's not always necessary to use the root note of a chord, in this case the D. The chord will still sound like a D—or a D7—even without the D being played. For the G triad that follows D7 in Phrase 1, I use G, B, and D—the notes that make up a G major chord.

So as the chords in "Whiskey Jug Rag" change, I just change my triad inversions and play the same rhythmic phrase. And I play it against the open string that is common to all the chords in the progression. That might sound like double-talk at the moment, but as we analyze the solo you'll see exactly what I'm talking about.

Why and When Open Strings Work

This open-string technique can be applied to all different kinds of progressions. One of the reasons it works real well for country music is because most country tunes are written in sharp keys, as opposed to flat keys. D and G are very common keys in country. So are E and A. These are all sharp keys—keys with sharps in the key signature you see at the beginning of each musical staff.

Diatonically, the open strings fit in the sharp keys and in the key of C (which has no sharps or flats). In the key of C, all six strings fit. All six strings are common to the key of C. The low E string is the 3rd of C. The A string is the 6th of C. The D string is the 2nd or 9th, G is the 5th, B is the major 7th, and the high E string is the 3rd. In the key of C, you can use any one of the six strings as an open string.

The next key in the cycle of 5ths is G. In the key of G, the low E is the 6th, A is the 2nd or 9th, D is the 5th, G is the root, B is the 3rd, and E is the 6th. In the key of D, the low E is the 2nd or 9th, A is the 5th, D is the root, G is the 4th, B is the 6th, and E is the 2nd or 9th. So all six open strings can be used in the keys of G and D.

The key of A is where it starts to get a little out there. In the key of A, the low E is the 5th, A is the root, D is the 4th, G is the dominant 7th, B is the 2nd or 9th, and E is the 5th. Because of the G string, you start getting dominant 7th licks, making the open-string licks start to sound kind of bluesy. But still, all six open strings can be used in the key of A.

As we go up the cycle of 5ths to the next key, the key of E, we get two "blue notes" as I call them. The E and A strings are diatonic. The D string is the dominant 7th, and the G string is a flat 3rd, another bluesy note. So the licks you'll play in E using open strings are going to start sounding even bluesier and less country-ish than in the key of A. But that's OK. I kind of like that sound.

That's why open strings work so well with the sharp keys.

The Solo

Phrase 1

Phrase 1 illustrates how I use an open string as part of a chord progression. The open E string will appear over both the D7 and G chords, and it will sound like it belongs in either chord. It's the 9th of the D7 chord and the 6th of the G chord. Later, you'll see how the open E is common to the other chords in the progression. That's one of the main rules in this technique, to use an open string that is common to all the chords in the progression.

Practice Point 1: I play a D7 chord with my fourth finger on F# at the 4th fret on the fourth string, my second finger on A at the 2nd fret on the third string, and my first finger on C at the 1st fret on the second string. I play F# with my pick, then A with my middle finger, and C with my ring finger. Then I play A with my pick, C with my middle finger, and the open E string with my ring finger. So I play strings 4, 3, and 2; then 3, 2, and 1. I repeat this, then play F♯ on string 4.

Practice Point 2: Then the chord changes to G. I play the same two-measure rhythmic phrase. The only thing that changes is the chord. I move my left hand up to 3rd position and play G at the 5th fret on the fourth string with my third finger, B at the 4th fret on the third string with my second finger, and D at the 3rd fret on the second string with my first finger. I use the open E with this chord as well.

Phrase 2

I move my triads up to different, higher inversions of the D7 and G chords for Phrase 2.

Practice Point 1: I move D7 up to play A at the 7th fret on the fourth string with my third finger, C at the 5th fret on the third string with my first finger, and F♯ at the 7th fret on the second string with my fourth finger. Again, I use the open E string in this chord. And again, I play strings 4, 3, 2; then 3, 2, 1. I repeat this, then play string 4 again.

Practice Point 2: I play B at the 9th fret on the fourth string with my third finger, D at the 7th fret on the third string with my first finger, and G at the 8th fret on the second string with my second finger, as well as open E. Same forward roll pattern with my right hand.

Do I Anchor My Right Hand?

Students often ask me if I use an anchor on my right hand. I don't anchor my right hand in the A section, when I play the forward banjo roll. I do use an anchor in the B section, and I'll describe that when we get to the B section. For the A section, I keep my right hand almost clenched like a fist. I tilt my wrist slightly downward so that my pick is hitting the strings at a forward angle. You lay your pick flat against your string and turn it forward like you are turning a key in a lock. Turn it to the point where the pick starts to slip off the string. That's the angle your right hand should be at. That will enable your middle and ring fingers to pull straight up. That saves nail wear, believe me.

Phrase 3

Phrase 3 is identical to Phrase 1.

Phrase 4

Phrase 4 takes us to an E and A minor change. Again, the open E string rings above and is common to both chords. The open E is the root of the E chord, and the 5th of the A chord.

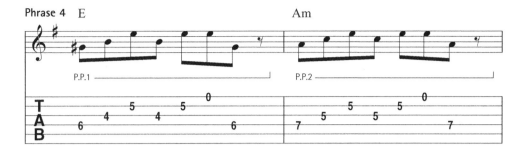

Practice Point 1: I use the same right-hand forward roll to play G♯ at the 6th fret on the fourth string with my fourth finger, B at the 4th fret on the third string with my first finger, and E at the 5th fret on the second string with my second finger. I also play the open E string. I pick strings 4, 3, 2, then 3, 2, 1, then string 4.

This fingering may seem a little awkward at first, but it's necessary to be able to quickly shift to the A minor chord in the next measure.

Practice Point 2: For the A minor chord, I slide my fourth finger up one fret to play A at the 7th fret on the fourth string, slide my first finger up one fret to play C at the 5th fret on the third string, leave my second finger on E on the second string, and, of course, play the open E string. This fingering is necessary to allow access to the open E string. Again, I pick strings 4, 3, 2, then 3, 2, 1, then string 4.

Phrase 5

Now I go back to one measure of D7 followed by one measure of G. This constitutes both the first and second ending of the A section. You've heard this phrase a lot. It's nothing more than a G scale, but played using open strings. I use the forward banjo roll to play the G scale, fitting in open strings wherever they fit diatonically.

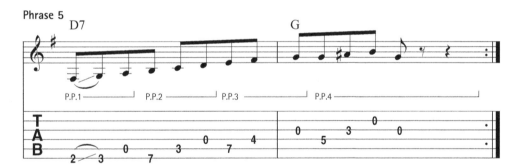

Practice Point 1: I play F♯ at the 2nd fret on the sixth string with my first finger, then slide it to G at the 3rd fret. Then I play A on the open fifth string. I play F♯ to G with my pick. I play the open fifth string (A) with my middle finger.

Practice Point 2: Now I stretch my left hand out to play B at the 7th fret on the sixth string with my fourth finger, C at the 3rd fret on the fifth string with my first finger, and D on the open fourth string. I play B with my pick, C with my middle finger, and D with my ring finger. Try to keep your left-hand fingers perpendicular to the strings so that all three strings can ring together. That sound is really important. It's like the effect you get at the piano when you push down the sustain pedal and play a scale, letting all the notes in the scale sustain together.

Practice Point 3: I play E at the 7th fret on the fifth string with my fourth finger, F♯ at the 4th fret on the fourth string with my first finger, and G on the open third string. Again, it's pick, middle finger, ring finger.

Practice Point 4: I end this phrase with something I call a "minor second" lick. They're very common in banjo music. I play G at the 5th fret on the fourth string with my fourth finger, B♭ at the 3rd fret on the third string with my first finger, and B on the open second string. Then I hit G on the open third string once more. This lick sounds dissonant and funky, but when you play it fast it sounds good. I play pick, middle finger, ring finger, then play the last G with my pick.

Phrase 6

Now let's take a look at the B section of this tune. The B section is considerably easier from a right-hand stand-point than the A section, because I don't use a full banjo roll; I don't use the pick, middle, and ring fingers. Instead, I use the pick and middle finger in an alternating motion. It only takes place on two strings, instead of three as in section A.

Overall, I employ the same technique, using a rhythmic phrase with the right hand and repeating that rhythmic phrase over all the chords in the progression. I repeat the rhythmic phrase against an open string that is common to all the chords in the progression. Again, I use the open high E as the common string.

Just as a reminder, the B section consists of one measure of C, one measure of A7, two measures of D7, two measures of G7, one measure of C, then a final measure broken into two beats of G7 and two beats of C. The open E string is the 3rd of the C chord. It's the 5th of A7. It's the 9th of the D7 chord, and the 6th of the G7 chord. That's why I chose the open E string.

My right hand plays almost entirely on the first and second string, until the end of the section. There is no roll involved; it's just pick and middle finger. My pick plays all the notes on the second string, and my middle finger plays all the notes on the first string. I just alternate between the first and second strings.

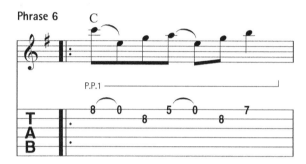

Practice Point 1: I start with my third finger on G at the 8th fret on the second string. My third finger is my anchor finger in this phrase; I hold it throughout the phrase. My fourth finger plays C at the 8th fret on the first string. I pluck C with my middle finger then pull off to the open E string. It's a big interval skip from C to open E.

You really have to pull off from C to E. You're going to play that C with your fourth finger, and you're going to have to yank it off the end of the fingerboard in order to get the open E to ring. Pull it straight down toward the floor; don't just lift it up off the string. You really want that open E to ring as loud as the other notes.

Then I play G on the second string. I let the open E and the G ring together. In fact, I let the G ring throughout the rest of the phrase. Then I play A at the 5th fret on the first string with my first finger. I pluck that note with my middle finger on my right hand, then pull off to open E again. Then I play G on the second string with my pick, then play B at the 7th fret on the first string with my second finger, plucking it with my middle finger. That's my rhythmic phrase.

Phrase 7

Now the chord changes to A7, so I can't play C♮. I have to raise that note to C♯. That gives me the sound of the A7.

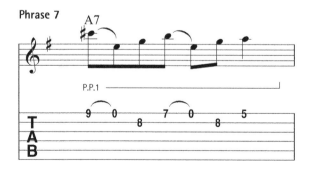

Practice Point 1: I play C♯ at the 9th fret on the first string with my fourth finger, plucking with my middle finger. I pull off to open E, then play G on the second string with my third finger and the pick. Again, I hold onto the G as my anchor note, letting it ring throughout the rest of the phrase.

Then I play B at the 7th fret on the first string with my second finger, then pull off to open E. Then I play G on the second string, then A at the 5th fret on the first string with my first finger. At the end of the phrase, I have A and G ringing together, which sounds a little discordant played slowly but works when you speed it up.

Phrase 8

Phrase 8 takes place over the D7 chord. It's a two-measure phrase. For this phrase I move my anchor note down one fret from G at the 8th fret on the second string to F♯ at the 7th fret. Now I can play the exact same phrase as in Phrase 6, with F♯ in place of G, and it sounds like a D7 chord.

Practice Point 1: I move my third finger down one fret to play F♯ at the 7th fret on the second string. I start with the C at the 8th fret on the first string, pull off to the open E, then play F♯ on the second string with the pick. I let the F♯ ring throughout the rest of the phrase.

Then I pull off from A to E, then play F♯ and B. I end the phrase with F♯ and C played together. I play F♯ with my pick and C with my middle finger.

Phrase 9

Now I play G7 for two measures. I lower the anchor note one more fret for this phrase.

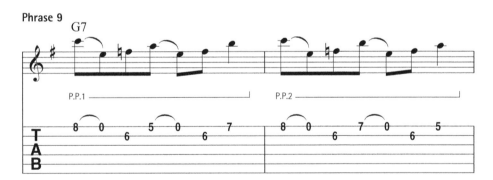

Practice Point 1: I replace F♯ on the second string with F♮ at the 6th fret, played with my second finger. This is now my anchor note. Now I play the same rhythmic phrase, with all the same notes, except for the F♮. That makes this phrase sound like G7.

I pull off from C to open E, play F♮, then pull off from A to open E. Then I play F, then B.

Practice Point 2: I just reverse a couple of notes in this part of the phrase. I pull off from C to open E, play F, then play B and pull off to open E. Then I play F and end on A.

Phrase 10

Now I play this cute little open-string lick. It's a ragtime lick that takes place on strings 3, 2, and 1—mostly on 2 and 1. I play all the notes on the first string with the middle finger on my right hand, and all the notes on the second and third strings with my pick.

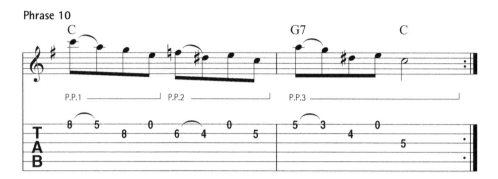

Practice Point 1: I start in 5th position. I pull off from C at the 8th fret on the first string with my fourth finger, to A at the 5th fret with my first finger. I pluck the first-string notes with my middle finger. Then I play G at the 8th fret on the second string with my third finger and the pick. Then I play open E with my middle finger again.

Practice Point 2: Then I slide down to 4th position and play F at the 6th fret on the second string with my third finger and the pick. I pull off to my first finger on D# at the 4th fret. Then I play open E with my middle finger. That's a minor 2nd interval. It sounds weird played slowly, but it's cool when you play it faster. Then I play C at the 5th fret on the third string with my second finger and pick.

Practice Point 3: Now I shift down to 3rd position and play A at the 5th fret on the first string with my third finger, plucking with my middle finger. I pull off from A to G at the 3rd fret, playing G with my first finger. Then I play D# on the second string with my second finger and pick, then open E, then play C on the third string with my third finger and pick.

Phrase 11

The B section repeats, just like the A section did. Phrase 11 is the second ending of the B section. It's nearly identical to Phrase 10, with a couple of notes missing.

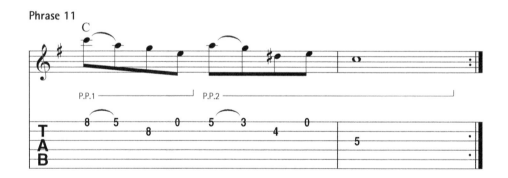

Practice Point 1: Identical to Phrase 10, Practice Point 1.

Practice Point 2: Identical to Phrase 10, Practice Point 3.

Understand the Concept

The whole idea behind this lesson and the entire ProLicks series is not so much to show you the licks—though I agree that they are all good and very useful, and that you should practice slowly and incorporate them into your playing. But it's more important that you understand the concept behind the licks. I want you to understand how and why I came up with these ideas. In other words, I want you to understand how I've just taken the progression that I have to solo over, and built or chosen triads underneath an open string that's common to all the chords in the progression.

This doesn't have to be done with just these chords—D7 to G. It can be done with any series of chords. It's a technique that is available to you in all different keys in all different places all over the neck. If you listen to guys like Chet Atkins and Jerry Reed, you're going to hear all kinds of different permutations of this same technique. Now that you understand how it works, you should have no trouble recognizing it on records.

Take what I've shown you here and, more than just learning and playing these licks, go back and analyze how I came up with them, and come up with your own licks. You'll incorporate this technique into your playing much faster if you come up with your own ideas rather than mine. I've given you a point of departure. Go ahead and fly.

5 Working Man's Licks

This chapter covers what I call "Working Man's Licks" or "Working Man's Country Guitar." What I mean by the phrase "working man" is, licks that sound very traditional and authentic—licks that have been played and recorded so many times over the years, they'll make you sound country by playing them even if you've never played country guitar in your life. Phrases such as those I'll show you in this chapter have been recorded by players such as Scotty Moore, James Burton, and Hank Garland. I stole a lot of the phrasing from these people.

I've taken a progression, the traditional working man's blues progression, which is a 12-bar blues in A, and I've worked out four choruses of phrases. So you can hear what these licks are going to sound like in the context of an actual musical progression.

Working Man's Licks

full band   minus guitar

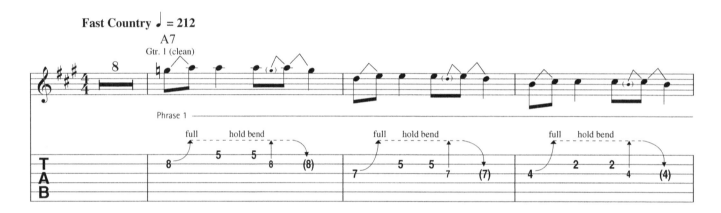

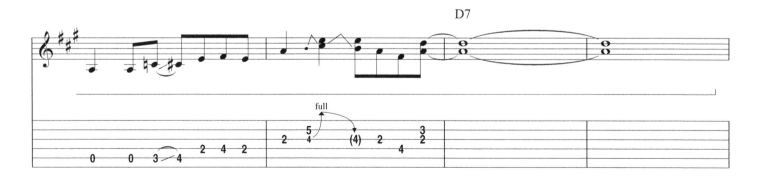

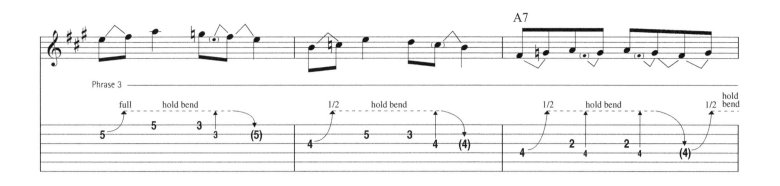

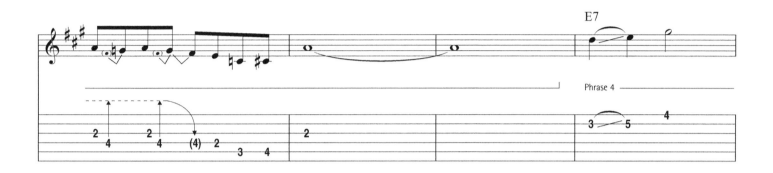

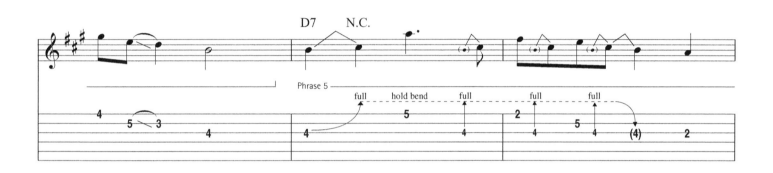

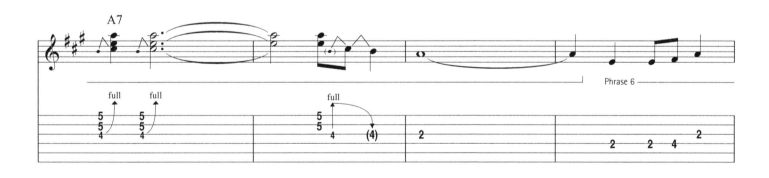

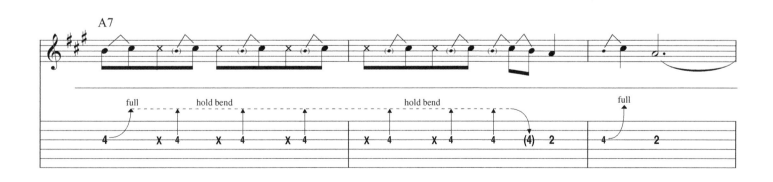

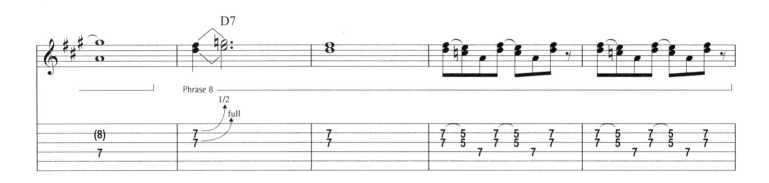

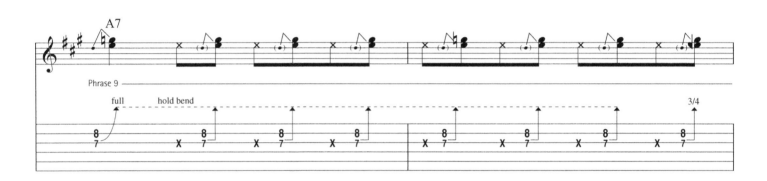

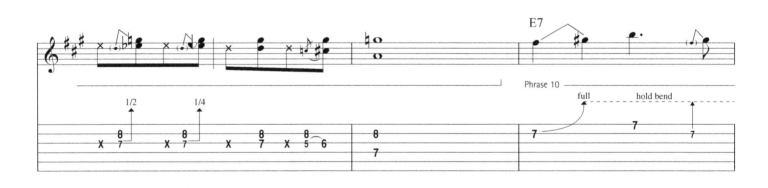

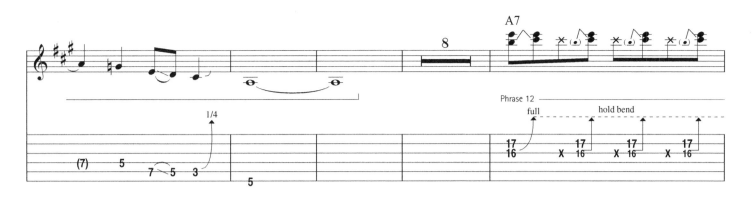

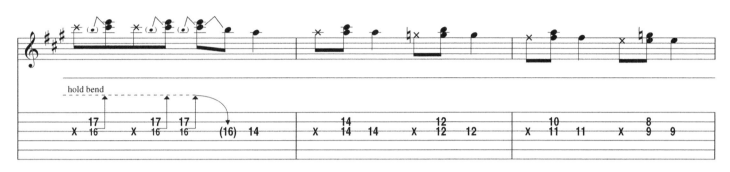

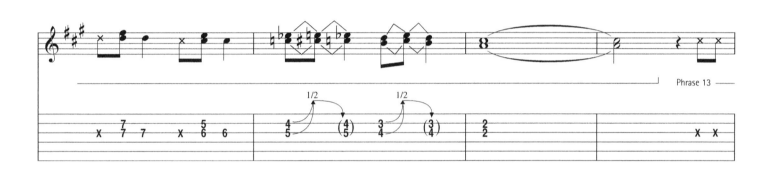

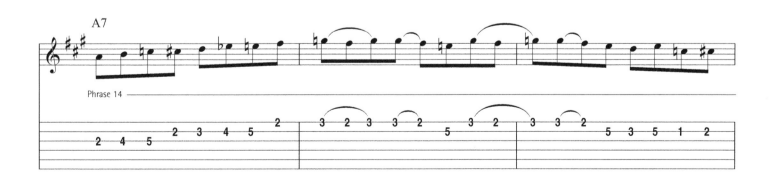

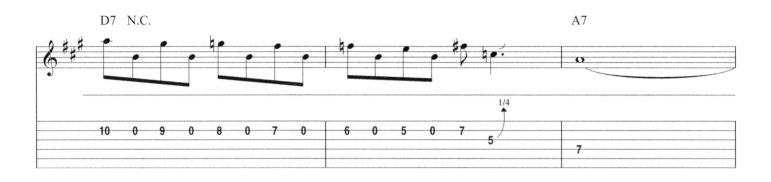

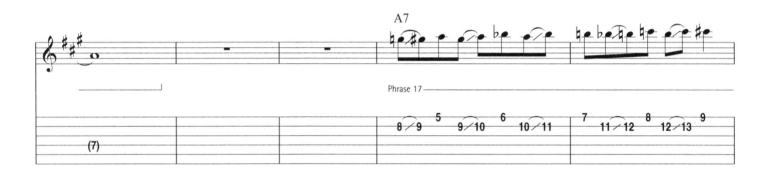

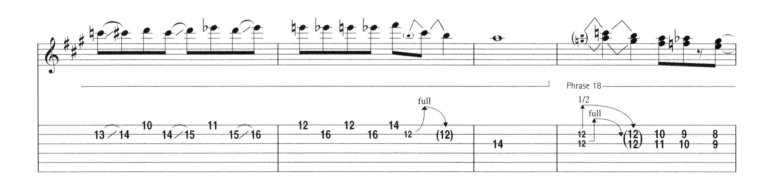

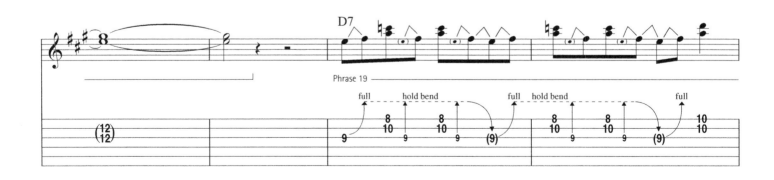

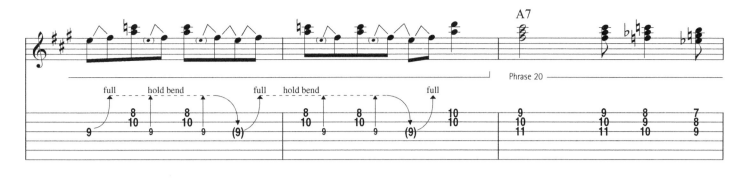

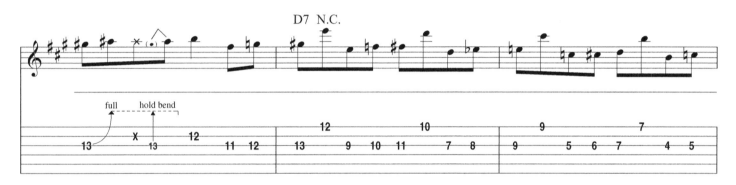

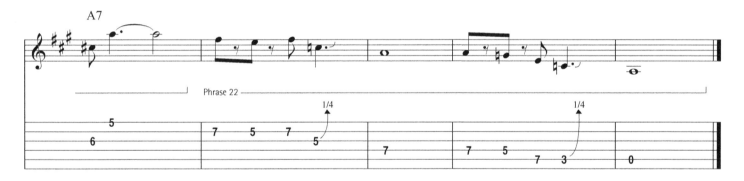

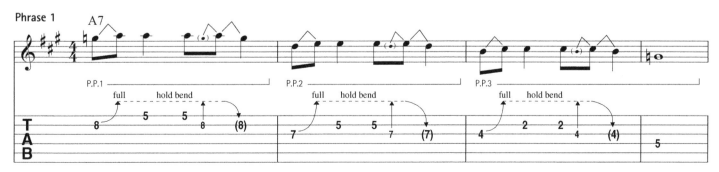

The Solo

Phrase 1

You've probably heard this lick many times.

Practice Point 1: I start in 5th position. I play G at the 8th fret on the second string with my fourth finger. I bend that note up a whole step to A. I bend over two eighth notes, then on the second beat of the measure, I play the unison A at the 5th fret on the first string with my first finger. On the third beat of the measure, I play the first string A again, then play the bent A on the second string and release it back to G. I hold the bent second string the whole time, until I release it at the end of the measure, letting the strings ring together.

Practice Point 2: Now I do the same thing on strings 3 and 2. I play D at the 7th fret on the third string with my third finger and bend it up a whole note to E, then play the unison E at the 5th fret on the second string with my first finger. Then I hit the E on the second string again, then play the bent E on the third string, then release it to D.

Practice Point 3: Then I move down to 2nd position and do the same thing, on the second and third strings. I play B at the 4th fret on the third string with my third finger, bend it up a whole step to C#, then play the unison C# at the 2nd fret on the second string with my first finger. I play the second string again, then play the bent third string, then release it. I end the phrase with G at the 5th fret on the fourth string with my fourth finger.

Phrase 2

Phrase 2 begins on the third and fourth strings.

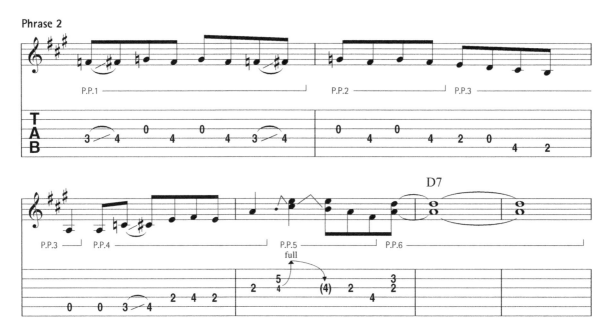

Practice Point 1: I play F at the 3rd fret on the fourth string with my third finger, then slide it up one fret to F# at the 4th fret. Then I play the open G string. I then play F#, G, F#. Then I do the slide again, from the 3rd to the 4th fret on the fourth string. I play all the notes on the fourth string with my pick, and the open G with the middle finger on my right hand. It's an alternating motion between my pick and middle finger, down with the pick, up with the finger. Also, I let the F# and G ring together.

Practice Point 2: I alternate between F# and G two more times.

Practice Point 3: I descend down a diatonic, A major scale. I play E at the 2nd fret on the fourth string with my first finger, then play the open fourth string. Then I play C# a the 4th fret on the fifth string with my third finger, B at the 2nd fret with my first finger, and open A.

Practice Point 4: I play the open A, then play C at the 3rd fret on the fifth string with my third finger, then slide up one fret to C# at the 4th fret. Then I play E at the 2nd fret on the fourth string with my first finger, F# at the 4th fret with my third finger, then E with first finger. Then I play A at the 2nd fret on the third string with my first finger.

Practice Point 5: I play B at the 4th fret on the third string with my third finger, and simultaneously play E at the 5th fret on the second string with my fourth finger. I play both notes together as a double stop. I then bend the B up a whole step to C#, while letting the E ring. I then release the bend, letting the B and E ring together. Then I play A at the 2nd fret on the third string with my first finger, still letting the E ring. Then, while holding those two notes, I play F# at the 4th fret on the fourth string with my third finger.

Practice Point 6: Then I play A on the third string with my first finger and D at the 3rd fret on the second string with my second finger. I play these notes together as a double stop. Whenever I play double stops, I play the lower note with my pick and the higher note with my middle finger. I pull them hard because I want that snap. That's the country sound.

Phrase 3

Phrase 3 takes place over the D chord, the IV (four) chord in the progression, and the A chord, the I (one) chord.

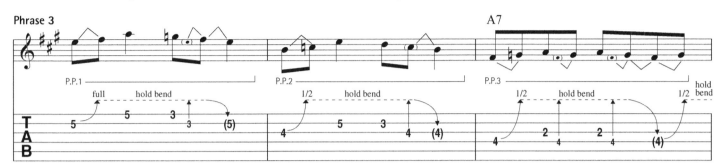

Practice Point 1: I start in third position. I play E at the 5th fret on the second string with my third finger, then bend it up a whole step to F♯. While holding the bend, I play A at the 5th fret on the first string with my fourth finger. Then while still holding the bend, I play G at the 3rd fret on the first string with my first finger. Then I hit the bent note and release it back to E.

Practice Point 2: Then I shift my third finger over to play B at the 4th fret on the third string. I bend that note a half step to C, then play E at the 5th fret on the second string with my fourth finger. I don't bend the B to C♯ because I'm playing over the D chord and I want the C♮, the dominant 7th of the D chord. Then I play D at the 3rd fret on the second string with my first finger. Then I hit the bent note and release it back to B.

Practice Point 3: Then I play F♯ at the 4th fret on the fourth string with my third finger and bend it up a half step to G. Then I play A at the 2nd fret on the third string with my first finger. I then play the G, then the A again. Then I play the G, release it to F♯, then bend it back to G.

Practice Point 4: Then I play A again, play G, A, G, and release to F♯. Then I play E at the 2nd fret on the fourth string with my first finger, then C at the 3rd fret on the fifth string with my second finger, then C♯ at the 4th fret with my third finger. Then I play A at the 2nd fret on the third string again.

Phrase 4

Now we get to the V (five) chord, the E7.

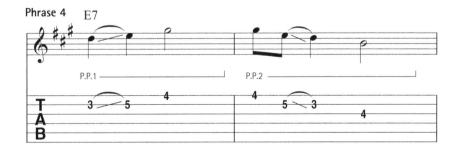

Practice Point 1: I play D at the 3rd fret on the second string with my second finger. I slide that finger to E at the 5th fret. Then I play G♯ at the 4th fret on the first string with my first finger.

Practice Point 2: Then I play G# again, hit E on the second string, slide it back to D, then play B at the 4th fret on the third string with my third finger.

Phrase 5

Here we go back to the last chord in the first chorus, the A or A7 chord. This is a pedal steel-type lick.

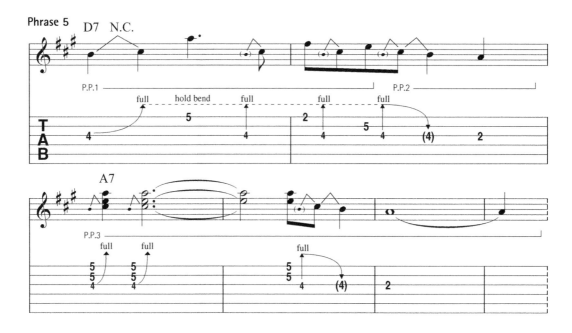

Practice Point 1: I play B at the 4th fret on the third string with my third finger, bend it up a whole step to C#, then play A at the 5th fret on the first string with my fourth finger. This is where it gets tricky. I hold that bend and play C#, then F# at the 2nd fret on the first string with my first finger, then C# again, then E at the 5th fret on the second string with my fourth finger, all while letting the bend ring.

Practice Point 2: Then I play C# again, release it to B, then play A at the 2nd fret on the third string with my first finger.

Practice Point 3: Then I grab the three top strings with my third finger on B at the 4th fret on the third string, and a fourth finger barre at the 5th fret across the first and second strings, to play E and A. I pluck those three strings while I bend B up to C#. I do this twice to get that pedal-steel sound. Then I pluck the three notes a third time, release the C# to B while I hold the notes, then play A at the 2nd fret on the third string with my first finger.

Phrase 6

I start the second chorus with a little chicken pickin'.

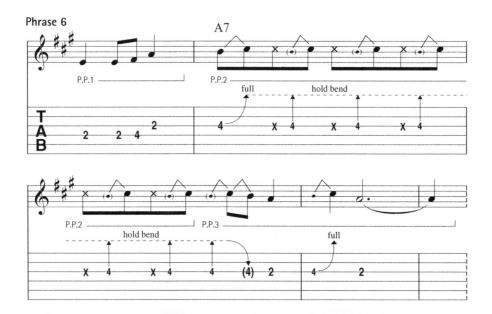

Practice Point 1: I play E at the 2nd fret on the fourth string with my first finger, then F# at the 4th fret with my third finger, then A at the 2nd fret on the third string with my first finger.

Practice Point 2: Then I play B at the 4th fret on the third string with my third finger. On the second half of beat 1, I bend that note up a step to C#. Then I start an alternating motion between my pick and the middle finger on my right hand. I play a picked note, muffled by tilting the pick downward so much that as I pick the note, my thumb on my right hand brushes against the string right after the pick. You can almost get a harmonic out of the string this way, but really you just want to muffle the note a little. Every time I pick it this way, I just get a percussive thump.

Then I play the same note with the middle finger on my right hand, but this time I let the note ring clearly. Then I alternate between these two sounds a few times, until halfway through the next measure.

Practice Point 3: Then I play the C# clearly, release to B, then play A at the 2nd fret on the third string with my first finger. After that, I play B on the third string, bend it quickly to C#, then play A again.

Phrase 7

I start Phrase 7 with the same little pickup, then get into a series of ascending bends and some cool double stops.

Practice Point 1: Identical to Phrase 6, Practice Point 1.

Practice Point 2: I play B at the 4th fret on the third string with my third finger, bend it up a whole step to C#, then play the unison C# at the 2nd fret on the second string with my first finger.

Practice Point 3: Then I slide up one fret and do the same thing. I play C♮ at the 5th fret on the third string with my third finger, bend it up a whole step to D, then play the unison D at the 3rd fret on the second string with my first finger. Then I slide it up one more fret and do the same thing, then another fret and bend D at the 7th fret up to E, and play the E unison at the 5th fret on the second string.

Practice Point 4: Then I play a double-stop bend. I play D at the 7th fret on the third string with my third finger and simultaneously play G at the 8th fret on the second string with my fourth finger. I play the D with my pick and the G with my middle finger. I bend the D up a whole step to E, while holding the G. Then I pluck the E and G together, then a second time, then release the E to D.

Practice Point 5: Then I play C at the 5th fret on the third string with my first finger, together with G, then hammer on C# at the 6th fret with my second finger. Then I play A at the 7th fret on the fourth string with my third finger, together with G.

Phrase 8

Phrase 8 includes a double-stop bend. When doing double-stop bends, you want to be very careful to keep both strings parallel to one another. Don't try to consciously bend one string differently than the other, even when the notes you're bending to are not the same distance from the starting notes.

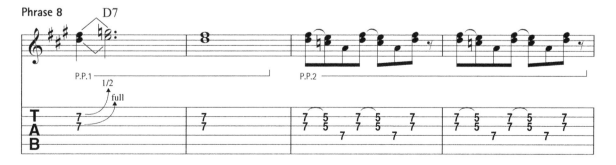

Practice Point 1: I play D at the 7th fret on the third string with my third finger and F# at the 7th fret on the second string with my fourth finger. I bend both notes together, the D up a whole step to E, and the F# up a half step to G. Concentrate on bending the D to E and just keep the F# parallel to that string, and it will go to the right place. Then I play the D and F# together without the bend.

Practice Point 2: Now I barre at the 7th fret across the second and third strings with my third finger. I play the D and F# together, then pull off to play C and E at the 5th fret on the second and third strings with my first finger. Then I play A at the 7th fret on the fourth string with my third finger. Then I repeat that lick one more time and end on the 7th-fret barre. And I repeat that entire lick a second time. I play the A on the fourth string with my pick and the notes on the second and third strings with the middle and ring fingers on my right hand.

Phrase 9

Now I go back to the I (one) chord, the A7 chord and some cool double-stop, chicken pickin' licks.

Practice Point 1: I play D at the 7th fret on the third string with my third finger, and at the same time G at the 8th fret on the second string with my fourth finger. I bend D up a whole step to E and play that double stop, alternating between a chicken pickin' technique and a clearly heard double stop. I play the chicken pickin' with a downstroke of the pick, muffled by my thumb. Then I pluck the double stop with the middle and ring fingers on my right hand. I only pick the third string when I get the muffled sound, but I play the second and third strings together with my right hand fingers. I play the bent E and the G together for one measure.

Practice Point 2: I continue to play the double stop, alternating with the chicken pickin', but each time I play the bent E on the third string, I lower it ever so slightly, so by the time I get through eight beats (two measures), it lowers back down to D. That gives me that kind of sleazy sound.

Practice Point 3: At the end of the phrase, I let go of the D and play C at the 5th fret on the third string with my first finger, together with G. Then I hammer on C#, then play A at the 7th fret on the fourth string with my third finger together with G.

Phrase 10

Phrase 10 is played over the E or V (five) chord in 5th position.

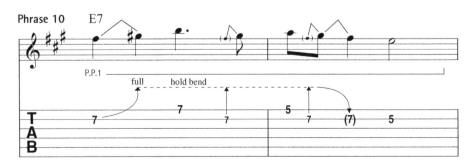

Practice Point 1: I play F♯ at the 7th fret on the second string with my third finger. Over two quarter notes, I bend the F♯ up a whole step to G♯, then play B at the 7th fret on the first string with my fourth finger while letting the bent note ring. Then I play the bent G♯ again, play A at the 5th fret on the first string with my first finger, then G♯ again. Then I release the G♯ to F♯, and then play E at the 5th fret with my first finger.

Phrase 11

Phrase 10 set me up for the open-string lick I play over the break in Phrase 11. The whole effect of an open-string lick is to let the strings ring together. It's supposed to sound like a cascading effect.

Practice Point 1: I start in 5th position fretting an A6 chord. I hold A at the 7th fret on the fourth string with my third finger, C♯ at the 6th fret on the third string with my second finger, F♯ at the 7th fret on the second with my fourth finger, and A at the 5th fret on the first string with my first finger.

I play A on the first string, F♯ on the second string, then the open first string, then F♯ again. I play the first string with the middle finger on my right hand and the second string with the pick. I alternate back and forth with the pick and middle finger on my right hand.

Practice Point 2: Then I play G at the 3rd fret on the first string with my first finger (a bit of a stretch), then F♯ on the second string, then the open first string, then C♯ on the third string. Again, I alternate between the pick and the middle finger on my right hand.

Practice Point 3: I skip over to the second and third strings now. I play F♯ on the second string, C♯ on the third string, the open second string, then A on the fourth string. Then I play C♯ and A again, then play the open third string. I end on A on the fourth string.

Practice Point 4: I let go of the A6 chord at this point and leave the open strings behind here. I play G at the 5th fret on the fourth string with my first finger, then E at the 7th fret on the fifth string with my third finger, slide down to D at the 5th fret, then play C at the 3rd fret with my first finger. I bend the C slightly to sound C♯, then play A at the 5th fret on the sixth string with my third finger.

Phrase 12

The third chorus starts an octave up, in 14th position, then moves down with double stops alternating with chicken pickin'.

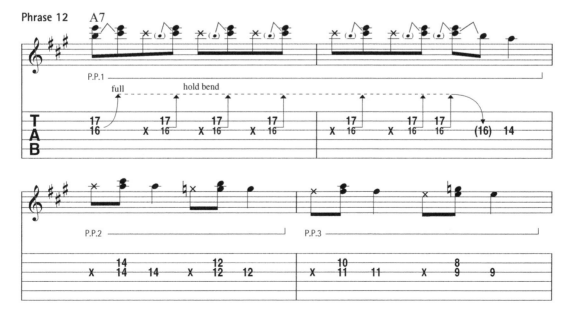

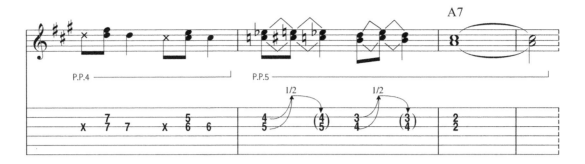

Practice Point 1: I play B at the 16th fret on the third string with my third finger, together with E at the 17th fret on the second string with my fourth finger. I play both notes together, then bend B up a whole step to C#. Then I do a chicken pickin' technique similar to the one I did in Phrase 9. I play the double stops with the middle and ring fingers on my right hand. In between those notes, I pick the third string, blocking the sound of the string with the middle finger on my right hand, creating a percussive thump. I alternate between the double stop and the thump. At the end of the phrase, I release the bend to B, then play A at the 14th fret on the third string with my first finger.

Practice Point 2: Then I barre at the 14th fret on the second and third strings with my first finger. First I play a thump with my pick, come back up across the double stop with my middle and ring fingers, then go down and play a picked third string again, but this time let it ring. Then I move my first finger down to the 12th fret, still barring the second and third strings, and do it again.

Practice Point 3: Then I play another thump, then play F# at the 11th fret on the third string with my third finger and A at the 10th fret on the second string with my second finger. Then I move down two frets to play E at the 9th fret on the third string with my third finger and G at the 8th fret on the second string with my second finger, after another percussive thump.

Practice Point 4: I keep moving down, alternating with the thump. This time, I play D at the 7th fret on the third string and F# at the 7th fret on the second string with a third-finger barre. Then I play C# at the 6th fret on the third string with my second finger and E at the 5th fret on the second string with my first finger.

Practice Point 5: I move down one more fret, to play C at the 5th fret on the third string with my second finger and E♭ at the 4th fret on the second string with my first finger. But this time I bend both notes up a half step, then release. Then I move down one more fret with the same shape, bend them up a half step, then release them. Then I finish the phrase with a first-finger barre at the 2nd fret on the second and third strings, where I play A and C#.

Phrase 13

Phrase 13 is a single-string lick in 5th position, played over the D or IV (four) chord. This lick is based in an A minor pentatonic pattern.

Phrase 13

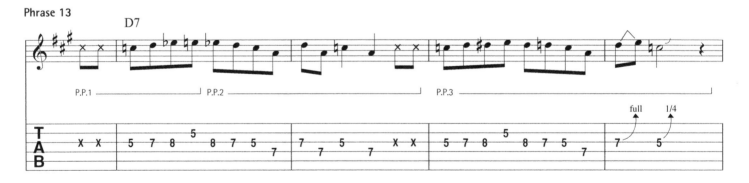

Practice Point 1: I play C at the 5th fret on the third string with my first finger, then D at the 7th fret with my third finger, then E♭ at the 8th fret with my fourth finger, then E at the 5th fret on the second string with my first finger.

Practice Point 2: Then I descend to E♭ on the third string, then D, C, and A at the 7th fret on the fourth string with my third finger. Then I play D on the third string, A on the fourth string, C on the third string, and A on the fourth string.

Practice Point 3: I repeat the same phrase, but instead of the ending that alternates between the third and fourth string, I just bend D up a whole step to E, choke it, then play C and give it a tug.

Phrase 14

Phrase 14 is played over an A chord and is based on an A major pentatonic in 2nd position. This phrase has an open-string effect without actually involving any open strings.

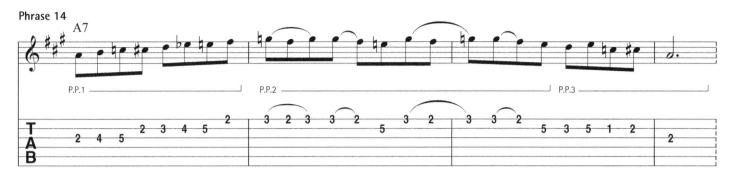

Practice Point 1: I play A at the 2nd fret on the third string with my first finger, B at the 4th fret with my third finger, C♮ at the 5th fret with my fourth finger, then C♯ at the 2nd fret on the second string with my first finger. I continue up the scale chromatically with D at the 3rd fret on the second string with my second finger, E♭ at the 4th fret with my third finger, E at the 5th fret with my fourth finger, and F♯ at the 2nd fret on the first string with my first finger. I hold the E on the second string while I play F♯ on the first string.

Practice Point 2: Then I play G at the 3rd fret on the first string with my second finger, pull off to F♯ at the 2nd fret with my first finger, hammer on to G again and play it twice, pull off to F♯ again, then play E at the 5th fret on the second string with my fourth finger. Then I repeat that lick.

Practice Point 3: I play D at the 3rd fret on the second string with my second finger, E at the 5th fret with my fourth finger, then reach down to play C at the 1st fret with my first finger, slide up one fret to play C♯ at the 2nd fret with my first finger, then play A at the 2nd fret on the third string with my first finger.

Phrase 15

Phrase 15 is another single-note lick, beginning in second position.

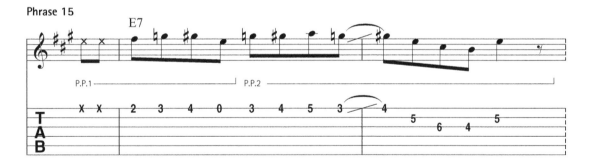

Practice Point 1: I play F♯ at the 2nd fret on the first string with my first finger, then G at the 3rd fret with my second finger, G♯ at the 4th fret with my third finger, then open E.

Practice Point 2: Then I move up to 3rd position and play G♮ with my first finger, G♯ with my second, and A at the 5th fret with my third finger. Then I play G♮ at the 3rd fret with my first finger, slide up one fret to G♯, then play E at the 5th fret on the second string with my second finger, C♯ at the 6th fret on the third string with my third finger, B at the 4th fret on the third string with my first finger, and E at the 5th fret on the second string with my second finger.

Phrase 16

Phrase 16 features a descending chromatic run alternating with an open string.

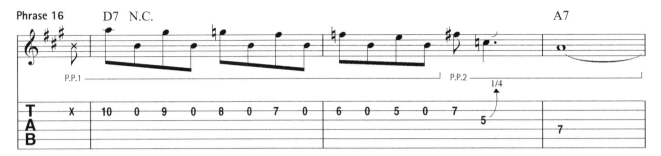

Practice Point 1: I play A at the 10th fret on the second string with my third finger, then the open second string. Then I play G♯ at the 9th fret with my second finger, then the open second string. I keep moving down chromatically, playing the open second string between each fretted note. I play G at the 8th fret, open, F♯ at the 7th fret, open, F♮ at the 6th fret, open, E at the 5th fret, open.

Practice Point 2: To finish the phrase, I play F♯ at the 7th fret with my third finger, then C at the 5th fret on the third string with my first finger, bend the C a little, then play A at the 7th fret on the fourth string with my third finger.

Phrase 17

Phrase 17 is a pedal-steel, slide kind of lick that you've heard pedal steel guitarists like Red Rhodes play. This is where the final chorus begins. This phrase takes place completely on the first and second strings.

Practice Point 1: I play G at the 8th fret on the second string with my fourth finger, then slide up one fret to G♯ at the 9th fret. Then I play A at the 5th fret on the first string with my first finger. I let the two strings ring together, creating dissonance. I use the pick on the second-string notes and the middle finger on my right hand on the first-string notes, in an alternating motion.

Practice Point 2: I keep my two left-hand fingers down, my fourth finger on G♯ and my first finger on A. I play G♯ with my fourth finger, then slide it up one fret to A at the 10th fret on the second string. As I slide my hand up one fret, my first finger slides up one fret to play B♭ at the 6th fret on the first string.

Practice Point 3: I make the same move three more times. I play A at the 10th fret on the second string, slide up to B♭ at the 11th fret, then play B♮ at the 7th fret on the first string with my first finger. Then I play B♭ on the second string, slide up to B♮ at the 12th fret, and play C at the 8th fret on the first string. The third time, I play B♮ at the 12th fret on the second string, slide to C at the 13th fret, then play C♯ at the 9th fret on the first string with my first finger. I hold on C♯ for one beat.

Practice Point 4: Then I continue the same movement another three times, moving up chromatically until, the third time, I play D at the 15th fret on the second string, slide up to E♭ at the 16th fret, then play E at the 12th fret on the first string.

Practice Point 5: I play E♭ at the 16th fret on the second string with my fourth finger, E at the 12th fret on the first string with my first finger, E♭ on the second string again, then F♯ at the 14th fret on the first string with my third finger. Then I pre-bend B at the 12th fret on the second string with my first finger up a whole step to C♯. I play the C♯, then release the note to B. Then I play A at the 14th fret on the third string with my second finger.

Phrase 18

Phrase 18 is a simple double-stop riff.

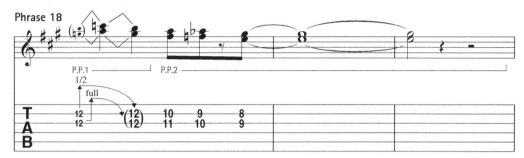

Practice Point 1: I pre-bend G at the 12th fret on the third string with my third finger and B at the 12th fret on the second string with my fourth finger. I bend G up a whole step to A and bend B up a half step to C♮ before I hit the strings. Concentrate on bending the second string, keep the strings parallel, and the third string will go where it's supposed to on its own. I hit the two notes, sounding the A–C double stop, then release them to the unbent G–B.

Practice Point 2: I play F♯ at the 11th fret on the third string with my third finger, together with A at the 10th fret on the second string with my second finger. Then I move that shape down one fret to play F♮ and A♭, then down another fret to play E at the 9th fret on the third string and G at the 8th fret on the second string.

Phrase 19

Phrase 19 is a standard pedal-steel lick in D.

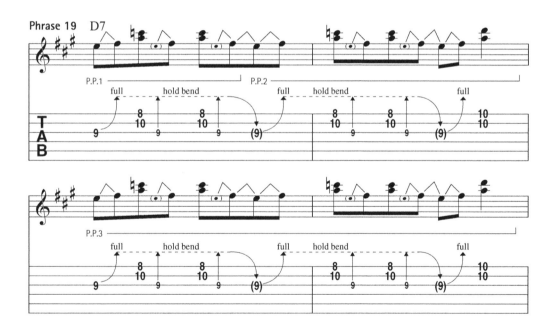

Practice Point 1: I play a fretted chord with C at the 8th fret on the first string with my first finger, A at the 10th fret on the second string with my fourth finger, and E at the 9th fret on the third string with my second finger. It looks like a C6 chord, but it is also a D9 chord. I bend the E up a whole step to F♯ on the third string, then play the A–C double stop together. Then I play the bent F♯ again. Then I play the double stop, followed by the bent F♯ again.

I use the middle and ring finger on my right hand to pluck the double stop, and the pick to play the third-string notes.

Practice Point 2: I play the lick again. I release the bent F♯ to E, play the E, then bend it back to F♯. I play double stop, F♯, double stop, F♯, release the bent F♯ to E, then bend it back to F♯. Then I lay my fourth finger down at the 10th fret across the first and second string and play A and D together.

Practice Point 3: Identical to Practice Points 1 and 2.

Phrase 20

Phrase 20 begins a series of descending A6 triads.

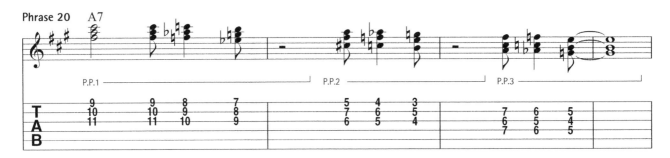

Practice Point 1: I start in 9th position with what amounts to an F♯ minor chord, or an A6 chord. I play C♯ at the 9th fret on the first string with my first finger, A at the 10th fret on the second string with my second finger, and F♯ at the 11th fret on the third string with my third finger. Then I move that shape down chromatically, first one fret, then another fret. I play the third string with my pick, the second string with my middle finger, and the first string with my ring finger. I grab the chord cluster the way a pedal steel player would. I cut the sound off quickly after the last chord.

Practice Point 2: I move to 5th position and play another A6 triad. I play A at the 5th fret on the first string with my first finger, F♯ at the 7th fret on the second string with my fourth finger, and C♯ at the 6th fret on the third string with my second finger. Then I move this triad down chromatically, first one fret, then another fret. I cut the sound off at the end.

Practice Point 3: Then I play an A6 triad on the second, third, and fourth strings. I play A at the 7th fret on the fourth string with my third finger, C♯ at the 6th fret on the third string with my second finger, and F♯ at the 7th fret on the second string with my fourth finger. I move that triad down chromatically as well, first one fret, then another fret. This time I let it ring at the end.

Phrase 21

Phrase 21 is the final E lick in the song.

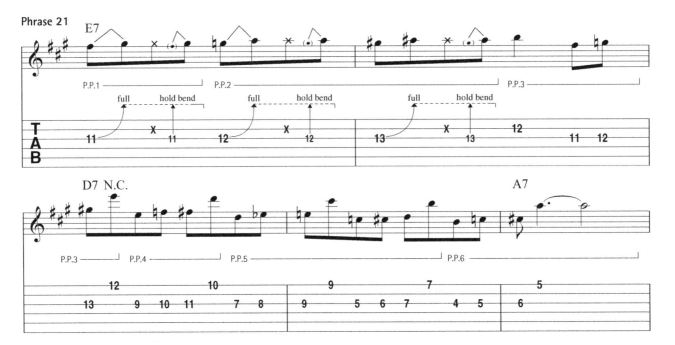

Practice Point 1: I start in 9th position and use my third finger to bend an F# at the 11th fret on the third string up a whole step to G#. I then play the unison G# at the 9th fret on the second string with my first finger, using a pick downstroke, but I muffle the string using the flesh of the middle finger on my right hand so I get the chicken pickin' effect. Then I come down and play the bent note on the third string normally with the pick.

Practice Point 2: I move up chromatically one fret and do the same thing as in Practice Point 1. Then I move up another fret and do it a third time.

Practice Point 3: I play B at the 12th fret on the second string with my second finger. Then I play F# at the 11th fret on the third string with my first finger, G at the 12th fret with my second finger, G# at the 13th fret with my third finger, and E at the 12th fret on the first string with my second finger. I play all the notes on the third string with my pick and all the notes on the first string with the middle finger on my right hand.

Practice Point 4: I move back to 9th position and do the exact same run as in Practice Point 3, this time beginning on E.

Practice Point 5: I move to 7th position and play D at the 7th fret on the third string with my first finger, D# at the 8th fret with my second finger, E at the 9th fret with my third finger, then play C# at the 9th fret on the first string with my fourth finger. Then I do the same exact run starting on C at the 5th fret on the third string and ending on B at the 7th fret on the first string.

Practice Point 6: Then I play B at the 4th fret on the third string with my first finger, C at the 5th fret with my second finger, C# at the 6th fret with my third finger, then A at the 5th fret on the first string with my second finger.

Phrase 22

I end the song over the last A chord with a funky, chicken pickin' lick.

Phrase 22

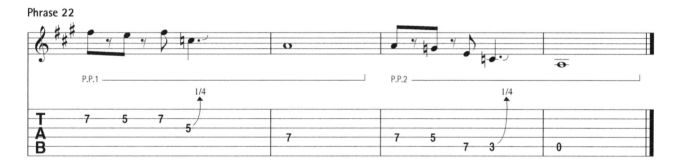

Practice Point 1: I play F# at the 7th fret on the second string with my third finger, then E at the 5th fret with my first finger, then F# again. Then I play C at the 5th fret on the third string with my first finger, give it a slight bend, then play A at the 7th fret on the fourth string with my third finger.

Practice Point 2: I play A at the 7th fret on the fourth string with my third finger, G at the 5th fret on the fourth string with my first finger, E at the 7th fret on the fifth string with my third finger, C at the 3rd fret on the fifth string with my first finger, then the open A string.

6 Flashy Country

In this chapter, I've pieced together licks in the style of two of my favorite artists, Albert Lee and Steve Morse. The solo is a sort of dueling, two-guitar situation. I play Albert Lee-style licks over a chorus of A, D, and E, then Steve Morse-style licks, then Lee, then Morse, and so on. You can plug in your own names; they're just licks, one in more of a standard country style, and one in more or less of a rock 'n' roll style, with distortion.

The Tone

The clean sound, the first solo, was my '61 Strat plugged into a Roland Chorus Echo, set for a quick slapback echo. I had a little reverb on it, and I had it set on the treble pickup. I played through an old Fender Pro Reverb amp with two JBL speakers. That's how I got the clean, Albert Lee sound. I also used a very staccato picking technique, which I'll talk more about later.

For the rock, Steve Morse-style sound, I used a double-coil pickup Paul Reed Smith guitar. I had that set on the bass pickup, and ran it through a Boss overdrive and a digital delay. The delay gives it a fatter sound. And I had the amp cranked up pretty loud. A couple of times in there when I played a note, you'd hear a weird harmonic that seemed to come out of nowhere. I would retract my pick up into my palm for those notes and play the note with just the tip of my pick. All I would get then would be a percussive thump and a harmonic. This is called chicken pickin'. The way to get the actual harmonic is, after you play the actual note with your pick, the string comes to rest on the side of your thumb. That's where the harmonic comes from.

Flashy Country

11 full band 12 minus guitar

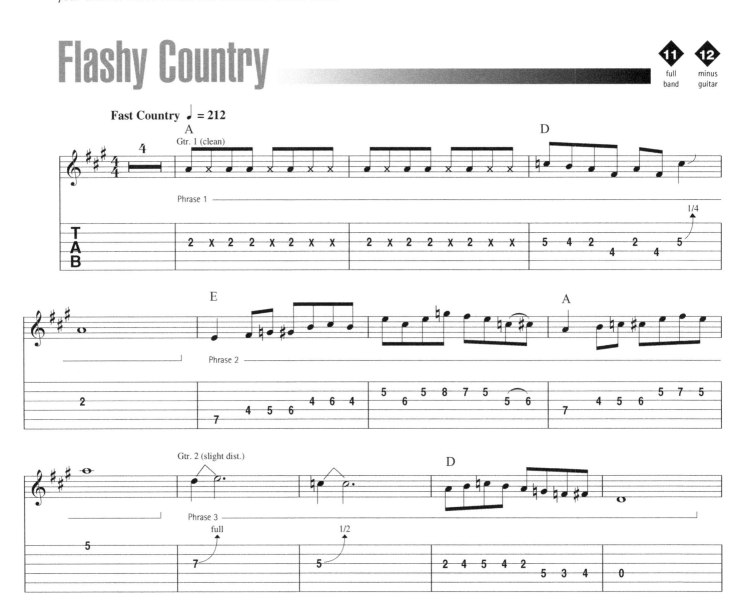

Fast Country ♩ = 212

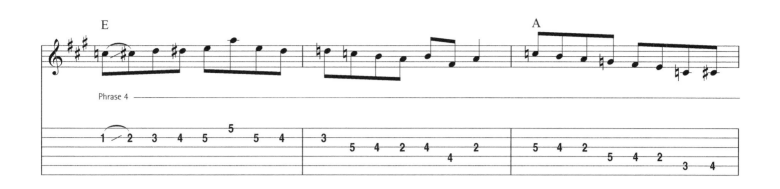

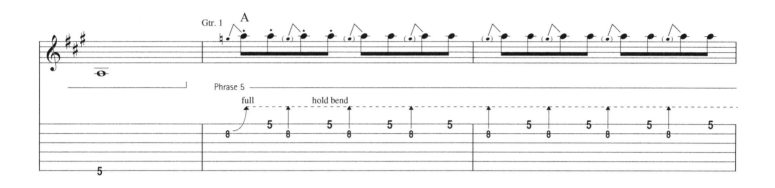

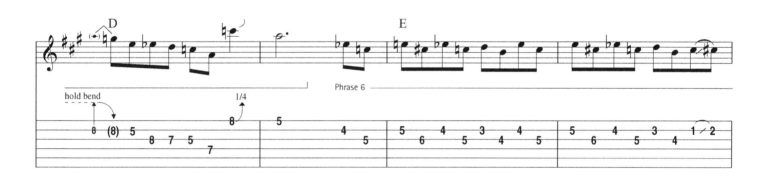

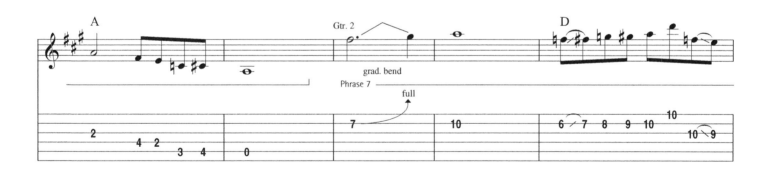

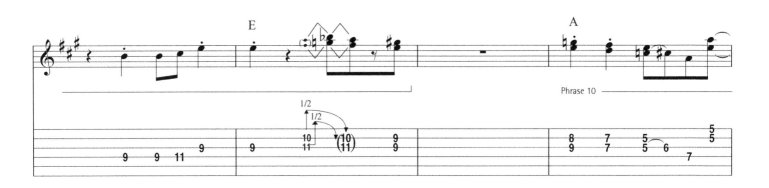

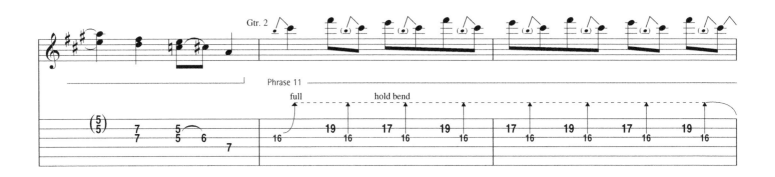

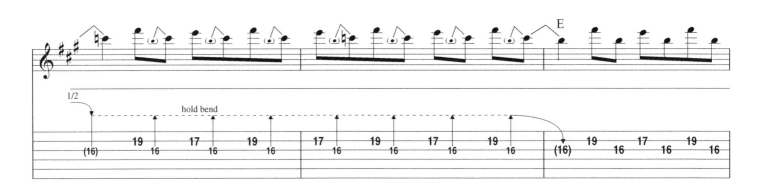

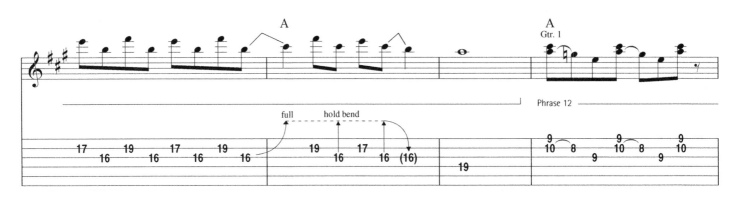

The Solo

Phrase 1

The solo starts with a clean, Albert Lee-style chicken pickin' lick.

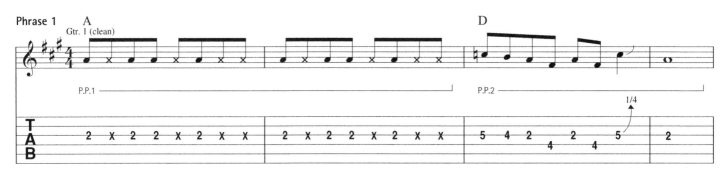

Practice Point 1: I play A at the 2nd fret on the third string with my first finger. I alternate between the pick and the middle finger on my right hand. When I pick the note, I come right up with the middle finger on my right hand and choke the note so it doesn't sound. Then I continue the up stroke with my middle finger to pick the note and let it ring. It's an alternating eighth note figure, played for two measures.

Practice Point 2: Then I play C at the 5th fret on the third string with my fourth finger, B at the 4th fret with my third finger, A at the 2nd fret with my first finger, then F# at the 4th fret on the fourth string with my third finger, then back to A, down to F# again, then C at the 5th fret on the third string again. I bend that C up a little, then play A again.

Phrase 2

I move up to 4th position to play a lick over an E chord.

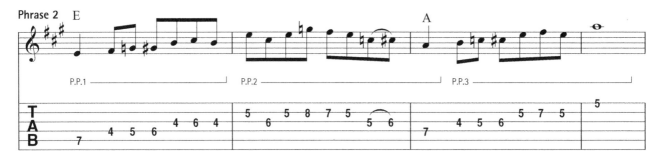

Practice Point 1: I play E at the 7th fret on the fifth string with my fourth finger. Then I play F# at the 4th fret on the fourth string with my first finger, G at the 5th fret with my second finger, and G# at the 6th fret with my third finger. Then I play B at the 4th fret on the third string with my first finger, C# at the 6th fret with my third finger, then B again.

Practice Point 2: I shift positions up one fret. I play E at the 5th fret on the second string with my first finger, C# at the 6th fret on the third string with my second finger, E again, then G at the 8th fret on the second string with my fourth finger. Then I play F# at the 7th fret with my third finger, E at the 5th fret with my first, then C♮ at the 5th fret on the third string with my first finger, hammer on C# at the 6th fret with my second finger, then play A at the 7th fret on the fourth string with my third finger.

Practice Point 3: I play B at the 4th fret on the third string with my first finger, C♮ at the 5th fret with my second finger, then C# at the 6th fret with my third finger. Then I play E at the 5th fret on the second string with my first finger, F# at the 7th fret with my third finger, E again, then A at the 5th fret on the first string with my first finger.

Phrase 3

On Phrase 3, I switch to the rock, Steve Morse-style sound.

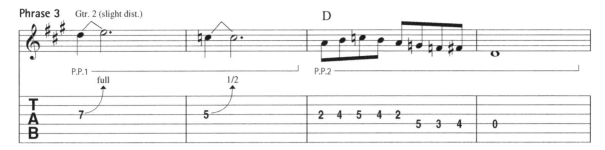

Practice Point 1: I play D at the 7th fret on the third string with my third finger, then bend it up a whole step to E. Then I play C♮ at the 5th fret on the third string with fourth finger and bend it up a half step to C♯. Each bend takes place over the length of a half note.

Practice Point 2: I play A at the 2nd fret on the third string with my first finger, then B at the 4th fret with my third finger, C at the 5th fret with my fourth finger, then down the scale: B, A, G at the 5th fret on the fourth string with my fourth finger, F♮ at the 3rd fret on the fourth string with my second finger, F♯ at the 4th fret with my third finger, then the open D string.

Phrase 4

Phrase 4 continues in the Steve Morse style.

Practice Point 1: I play C♮ at the 1st fret on the second string with my first finger, slide up one fret to C♯, then play D at the 3rd fret with my second finger, D♯ at the 4th fret with my third finger, then E at the 5th fret with my fourth finger. Then I flop my fourth finger over to play A at the 5th fret on the first string.

Practice Point 2: I come back down, playing E at the 5th fret on the second string with my fourth finger, D♯ at the 4th fret with my third finger, D♮ at the 3rd fret with my second finger. Then I play C at the 5th fret on the third string with my fourth finger, B at the 4th fret with my third finger, A at the 2nd fret with my first finger. Then I play B again, then F♯ at the 4th fret on the fourth string with my third finger, then A again.

Practice Point 3: I play C at the 5th fret on the third string with my fourth finger, then B at the 4th fret, A at the 2nd fret. Then I move over to the fourth string and play G at the 5th fret on the fourth string, F♯ at the 4th fret with my third finger, E at the 2nd fret with my first finger. Then I play C at the 3rd fret on the fifth string with my second finger, C♯ at the 4th fret with my third finger, then A at the 5th fret on the sixth string with my fourth finger.

On this last note, I get the weird harmonics by holding the pick real tight in my right hand, with just the tip of the pick showing, and as I pick the note I let the flesh of my finger brush the string. That's when the harmonic pops out. A lot of the time, it's just luck when you get that harmonic, but it sounds good.

Phrase 5

Phrase 5 alternates back to the Albert Lee-style again.

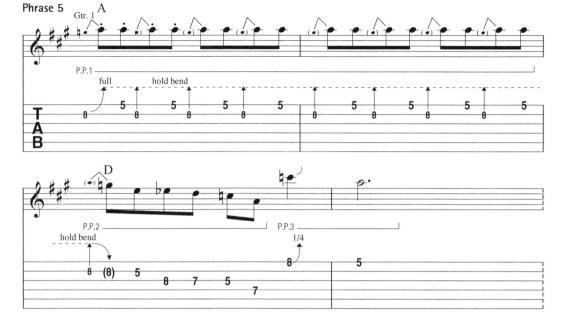

Practice Point 1: I play G at the 8th fret on the second string with my fourth finger, bend it up a whole step to A. Then I play staccato eighth notes, alternating with the unison A at the 5th fret on the first string with my first finger. I play second string A, first string A, second string A, etc. I do that for two measures.

Practice Point 2: Then I release the bend and play G at the 8th fret on the second string with my fourth finger, E at the 5th fret with my first finger, then E♭ at the 8th fret on the third string with my fourth finger, D at the 7th fret with my third finger, C at the 5th fret with my first finger, then A at the 7th fret on the fourth string with my third finger.

Practice Point 3: Then I shift back up, as Albert Lee is known to do, and play C at the 8th fret on the first string with my fourth finger. I bend the note up just a little, then play A at the 5th fret with my first finger.

Phrase 6

With both of these styles of playing, the Albert Lee-style and the Steve Morse-style, I've found that it works better if you pick every note. If you try to slur the notes, it loses a lot in the translation. If you listen closely to guys like Steve Morse, Albert Lee, Jerry Reed, and Ray Flacke—guys who play fast like that—you'll notice that, for the most part, they're picking every note. That's what gives the characteristic sound. So remember that when you're practicing these. Don't try to slur notes. You'll notice the difference right away.

Practice Point 1: I use an alternating motion between the pick and the middle finger on my right hand. The lick takes place on the second and third string, so my pick plays all the notes on the third string, and my middle finger plays all the notes on the second string.

The left-hand fingering is very important for this lick as well. I play E♭ at the 4th fret on the second string with my second finger, then C♮ at the 5th fret on the third string with my third finger. Then I move up one fret and play E at the 5th fret on the second string with my second finger, then C♯ at the 6th fret on the third string with my third finger. Then I move down one fret and play E♭ on the second string and C♮ on the third string. Then I move down one more fret and play D on the second string and B on the third string. Then I move back up one fret to play E♭ and C again.

Practice Point 2: I play E and C# again, then E♭ and C♮, then D and B, just like in Practice Point 1. Then I shift my left hand to first position and play C♮ at the 1st fret on the second string with my first finger, then slide my first finger up one fret to play C# at the 2nd fret. Then I play A at the 2nd fret on the third string with my first finger.

Practice Point 3: The tag on the end of the lick starts with F# at the 4th fret on the fourth string with my third finger, E at the 2nd fret with my first finger, then C♮ at the 3rd fret on the fifth string with my second finger, C# at the 4th fret with my third finger, and then the open A string.

Phrase 7

That brings us to the second Steve Morse-style, or country rock-type, chorus.

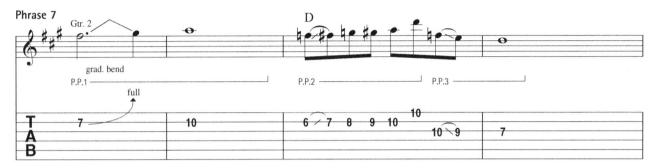

Practice Point 1: I start in 7th position. I play F# at the 7th fret on the second string with my first finger and bend it up, then play A at the 10th fret with my fourth finger. That sets me up for the next lick, which happens over a D chord.

Practice Point 2: I play F♮ at the 6th fret on the second string with my first finger. I slide up one fret to F#, then play G at the 8th fret with my second finger, then G# at the 9th fret with my third finger. Then I play A at the 10th fret with my fourth finger, then lay my fourth finger down across the first and second strings at the 10th fret and play D on the first string.

Practice Point 3: I play F at the 10th fret on the third string with my third finger, then slide down one fret to play E at the 9th fret, then play D at the 7th fret with my first finger.

Phrase 8

I shift up to 13th position to play Phrase 8 over the E chord. This is a three- and four-note sequence.

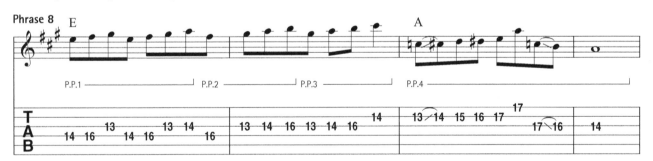

Practice Point 1: I play E at the 14th fret on the fourth string with my second finger, then F# at the 16th fret with my fourth finger, then G# at the 13th fret on the third string with my first finger. Then I repeat those three notes, then play A at the 14th fret on the third string with my second finger.

Practice Point 2: I play F# at the 16th fret on the fourth string with my fourth finger, then G# at the 13th fret on the third string with my first finger, A at the 14th fret with my second finger, and B at the 16th fret with my fourth finger.

Practice Point 3: I play G# at the 13th fret on the third string with my first finger, A with my second finger, B with my fourth finger, then C# at the 14th fret on the second string with my first finger.

Practice Point 4: Now I play the same lick I played in Phrase 7, Practice Points 2 and 3, but this time I do it over an A chord. I play C at the 13th fret on the second string with my first finger, slide up one fret to play C# at the

14th fret, play D at the 15th fret with my second finger, then D# at the 16th fret with my third finger. Then I play E at the 17th fret with my fourth finger, and lay my fourth finger across the first and second strings to play A at the 17th fret on the first string.

Then I play C at the 17th fret on the third string with my third finger, slide down one fret to play B at the 16th fret, then play A at the 14th fret with my first finger.

Phrase 9

Now I go back to the next Albert Lee or clean country-style lick. This phrase is a series of parallel licks moving over the triads of A, D, and E. Albert Lee plays a lot with his pick and the middle and ring fingers of his right hand. On Phrase 9, I alternate between parts that are picked and sound kind of like chicken pickin', and parts that are plucked with the fingers of the right hand, which sound more like Albert Lee.

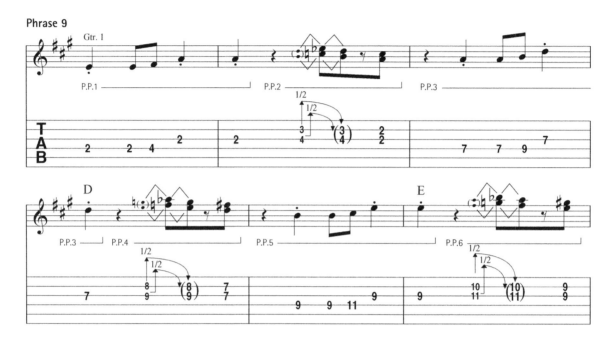

Practice Point 1: I play E at the 2nd fret on the fourth string with my first finger, play it again, then hit F# at the 4th fret with my third finger, then A at the 2nd fret on the third string with my first finger. I hit A twice.

Practice Point 2: I finger B at the 4th fret on the third string with my third finger and D at the 3rd fret on the second string with my second finger. Before I hit the strings, I pre-bend those notes up a half step to play C and E♭. I use the middle and ring fingers on my right hand to pluck the notes. Then I release the notes to B and D. Then I play A at the 2nd fret on the third string and C# at the 2nd fret on the second string with a first-finger barre.

Practice Point 3: For the D chord, I take that same lick, shift it up to 7th position, and play exactly the same thing. You'll notice that the double stops get easier to bend up higher on the neck. First I play A at the 7th fret on the fourth string with my first finger, hit it again, then play B at the 9th fret with my third finger, then D at the 7th fret on the third string with my first finger twice.

Practice Point 4: Then I do the double stops. I finger E at the 9th fret on the third string with my third finger and G at the 8th fret on the second string with my second finger, and pre-bend them up a half step to play F# and A♭. I pluck those strings with my ring and middle finger, release the notes to E and G, then play D and F# at the 7th fret on the second and third strings with a first-finger barre. Ideally, you want to bend the double stop up a half step, but if you can't that's OK. Just bend them up somewhere and let them come back, so that you get the feeling and the sound of a bend.

Practice Point 5: Now I move the lick up to play over the E chord. I play B at the 9th fret on the fourth string with my first finger, hit it again, then play C# at the 11th fret with my third finger, then E at the 9th fret on the third string with my first finger twice.

Practice Point 6: I finger F# at the 11th fret on the third string with my third finger and A at the 10th fret on the second string with my second finger. I pre-bend both notes up a half step to play G and B♭, pluck them with my middle and ring finger, release them to play F# and A, then play the first-finger barre across the second and third strings at the 9th fret to play E and G#.

Phrase 10

Phrase 10 is the tag for Phrase 9. In this lick, the only time I use my pick is on the fourth string.

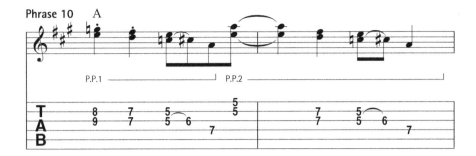

Practice Point 1: I play E at the 9th fret on the third string with my third finger, G at the 8th fret on the second string with my second finger. Then I shift down to 5th position and barre my third finger across the second and third strings at the 7th fret to play D and F#. Then I play a first-finger barre at the 5th fret to play C and E, then hammer on C# at the 6th fret with my second finger. Then I play A at the 7th fret on the fourth string with my third finger. I play all the double stops in this lick with the middle and ring fingers on my right hand. I play all the third-string notes with my middle finger and all the second-string notes with my ring finger. I play on the fourth string with my pick.

Practice Point 2: I play a first-finger barre at the 5th fret on the first and second strings to play E and A. Then I do the second half of Practice Point 1. I play the 7th-fret barre, the 5th-fret barre, hammer on the C#, then play A on the fourth string with my pick.

Phrase 11

I move up to 16th position to play the fourth Steve Morse, or maybe Eric Johnson, rock-style solo. In this particular lick, the right hand is going to require a very fast alternate motion between the pick and the middle finger. That's how I get the chicken pickin' effect. The lick takes place on the second and third strings. I play all the notes on the third string with my pick, and all the notes on my second string with my middle finger. It's all alternating motion.

To get this phrase to sound like a barnyard animal of some sort, you have to muffle the strings. I use the heel of my right hand, right almost on the bridge. You want the strings to sound, to ring out, but just not all the way. Don't mute them so much that they sound like just percussive thumps; let them ring out a little.

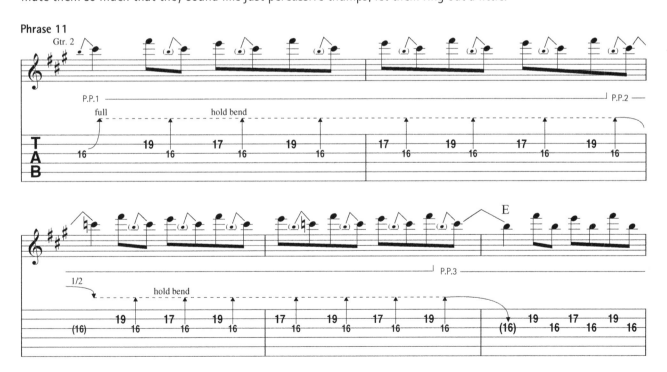

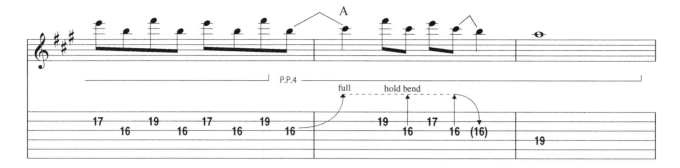

Practice Point 1: I play B at the 16th fret on the third string with my first finger, then bend it up a whole step to C♯. I bend up toward the ceiling, hold the bend, then add F♯ at the 19th fret on the second string with fourth finger. Then I play the bent C♯, then E at the 17th fret on the second string with my second finger. Throughout this part of Phrase 11, I hold the bent C♯ and alternate between F♯ and E on the top very rapidly.

Practice Point 2: When I get to the D7 chord, I let the C♯ down a half step to C♮, and continue with the F♯ and E on top. So now I'm only bending the B up a half step to C♮.

Practice Point 3: When the band plays the E chord, I let the bent third string resolve down to its original pitch, B at the 16th fret. I continue with the F♯ and E on top.

Practice Point 4: I bend the B back up to C♯, play the F♯ on top, then E on top, release the bend to B, then play A at the 19th fret on the fourth string with my third finger.

Phrase 12

Phrase 12 is another clean, Albert Lee or Ray Flacke -style part, played off an A triad in 8th position.

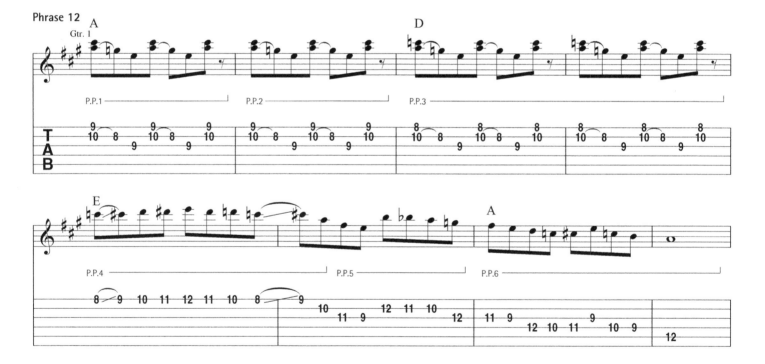

Practice Point 1: I play an A triad on the top three strings. I play E at the 9th fret on the third string with my second finger, A at the 10th fret on the second string with my fourth finger, and C♯ at the 9th fret on the first string with my third finger. Because it's doing nothing, my first finger rests on G at the 8th fret on the second string. I'll use it in a moment. I play all the notes on the first string with my ring finger, all the notes on the second string with my middle finger, and all the notes on the third string with my pick.

I pluck A and C♯ with my middle and ring fingers, then pull off from A to G on the second string. Then I play E on the third string with my pick. I repeat this one time, then end with the A and C♯ together.

Practice Point 2: Identical to Practice Point 1.

Practice Point 3: I lower the C♯ to C to play over the D7 triad. I play E and A the same as before, with my second and fourth finger, respectively. I barre my first finger across the top two strings at the 8th fret to play G on the second string and C on the first string. My right hand plays exactly the same rhythm as in Practice Point 1, and my left hand does the same pull-off from A to G.

Practice Point 4: I finish the phrase with a trademark Albert Lee-style, single-note run. This is all out of the fingering pattern for an A chord at the 9th position. I play C at the 8th fret on the first string with my first finger, slide up one fret to play C♯, then play chromatically up to E at the 12th fret—C♯, D, D♯, E. Then I come back down to D♯, D, then play C♮, slide up to C♯, and play A at the 10th fret on the second string with my second finger.

Practice Point 5: I play F♯ at the 11th fret on the third string with my third finger, E at the 9th fret with my first finger, then B at the 12th fret on the second string with my fourth finger, B♭ at the 11th fret with my third finger, A at the 10th fret with my second finger, and G at the 12th fret on the third string with my fourth finger.

Practice Point 6: I continue down the scale with F♯ at the 11th fret with my third finger, E at the 9th fret with my first finger, then D at the 12th fret on the fourth string with my fourth finger, C at the 10th fret with my second finger, C♯ at the 11th fret with my third finger, and E at the 9th fret on the third string with my first finger. Then I play C at the 10th fret on the fourth string with my second finger, B at the 9th fret with my first finger, and A at the 12th fret on the fifth string with my fourth finger.

Phrase 13

This brings us to the last chorus of the country rock, Steve Morse, or Billy Gibbons-style—whomever you want to name it after—solo. I play this in the 17th position.

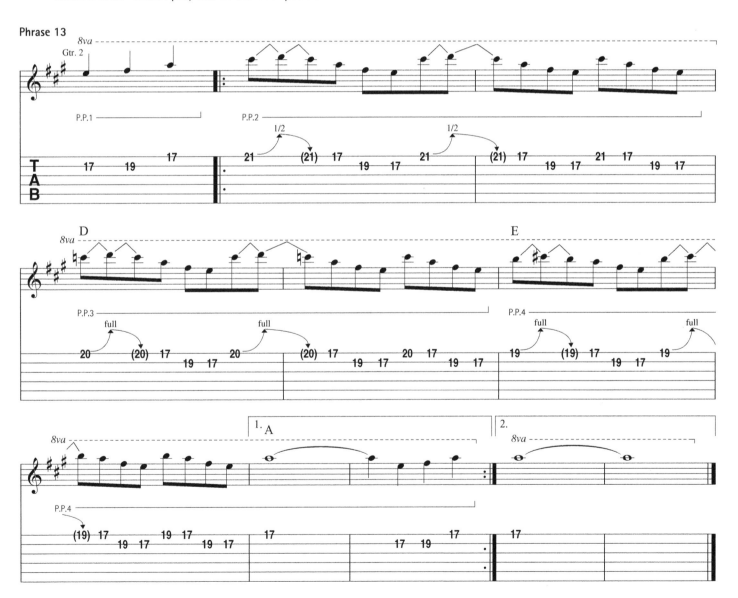

Practice Point 1: I play E at the 17th fret on the second string with my first finger, then F# at the 19th fret with my third finger, then A at the 17th fret on the first string with my first finger.

Practice Point 2: Then I play C# at the 21st fret on the first string with my fourth finger. It's way up there. I play the C#, then bend it up a half step to D, then release it to C#, all very quickly. I only pick the note once. Then I play A at the 17th fret with my first finger, then F# at the 19th fret on the second string with my third finger, and E at the 17th fret with my first finger. If it's more comfortable, you can play the F# with your second finger. I repeat this lick twice, and then a third time without the bend.

Practice Point 3: The chord changes to D at this point, so I lower my top note one fret to C♮ at the 20th fret. I do the same exact lick as in Practice Point 2, except I bend from C♮ up a whole step to D.

Practice Point 4: Then I play the lick exactly the same again, except I play B at the 19th fret, bend it up to C#, release it to B, then play the lower notes.

I repeat Practice Points 1 through 4 to end the solo.

That's All, Folks

I hope you've enjoyed this book and benefited from it. Remember: Practice slowly, be patient, work hard, and have fun.

Guitar Notation Legend

Guitar Music can be notated three different ways: on a *musical staff*, in *tablature*, and in *rhythm slashes*.

RHYTHM SLASHES are written above the staff. Strum chords in the rhythm indicated. Use the chord diagrams found at the top of the first page of the transcription for the appropriate chord voicings. Round noteheads indicate single notes.

THE MUSICAL STAFF shows pitches and rhythms and is divided by bar lines into measures. Pitches are named after the first seven letters of the alphabet.

TABLATURE graphically represents the guitar fingerboard. Each horizontal line represents a string, and each number represents a fret.

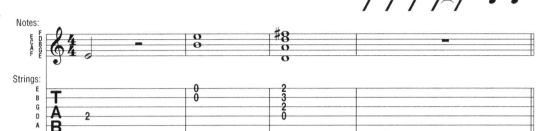

4th string, 2nd fret   1st & 2nd strings open, played together   open D chord

HALF-STEP BEND: Strike the note and bend up 1/2 step.

WHOLE-STEP BEND: Strike the note and bend up one step.

GRACE NOTE BEND: Strike the note and bend up as indicated. The first note does not take up any time.

SLIGHT (MICROTONE) BEND: Strike the note and bend up 1/4 step.

BEND AND RELEASE: Strike the note and bend up as indicated, then release back to the original note. Only the first note is struck.

PRE-BEND: Bend the note as indicated, then strike it.

VIBRATO: The string is vibrated by rapidly bending and releasing the note with the fretting hand.

WIDE VIBRATO: The pitch is varied to a greater degree by vibrating with the fretting hand.

HAMMER-ON: Strike the first (lower) note with one finger, then sound the higher note (on the same string) with another finger by fretting it without picking.

PULL-OFF: Place both fingers on the notes to be sounded. Strike the first note and without picking, pull the finger off to sound the second (lower) note.

LEGATO SLIDE: Strike the first note and then slide the same fret-hand finger up or down to the second note. The second note is not struck.

SHIFT SLIDE: Same as legato slide, except the second note is struck.

TRILL: Very rapidly alternate between the notes indicated by continuously hammering on and pulling off.

TAPPING: Hammer ("tap") the fret indicated with the pick-hand index or middle finger and pull off to the note fretted by the fret hand.

NATURAL HARMONIC: Strike the note while the fret-hand lightly touches the string directly over the fret indicated.

PINCH HARMONIC: The note is fretted normally and a harmonic is produced by adding the edge of the thumb or the tip of the index finger of the pick hand to the normal pick attack.

PICK SCRAPE: The edge of the pick is rubbed down (or up) the string, producing a scratchy sound.

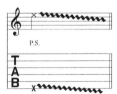

MUFFLED STRINGS: A percussive sound is produced by laying the fret hand across the string(s) without depressing, and striking them with the pick hand.

PALM MUTING: The note is partially muted by the pick hand lightly touching the string(s) just before the bridge.

RAKE: Drag the pick across the strings indicated with a single motion.

TREMOLO PICKING: The note is picked as rapidly and continuously as possible.

VIBRATO BAR DIVE AND RETURN: The pitch of the note or chord is dropped a specified number of steps (in rhythm) then returned to the original pitch.

VIBRATO BAR SCOOP: Depress the bar just before striking the note, then quickly release the bar.

VIBRATO BAR DIP: Strike the note and then immediately drop a specified number of steps, then release back to the original pitch.

Get Better at Guitar

...with these Great Guitar Instruction Books from Hal Leonard!

101 GUITAR TIPS
INCLUDES TAB

STUFF ALL THE PROS KNOW AND USE

by Adam St. James

This book contains invaluable guidance on everything from scales and music theory to truss rod adjustments, proper recording studio set-ups, and much more.

00695737 Book/Online Audio $16.99

AMAZING PHRASING
INCLUDES TAB

by Tom Kolb

This book/audio pack explores all the main components necessary for crafting well-balanced rhythmic and melodic phrases. It also explains how these phrases are put together to form cohesive solos. The companion audio contains 89 demo tracks, most with full-band backing.

00695583 Book/Online Audio $19.99

ARPEGGIOS FOR THE MODERN GUITARIST
INCLUDES TAB

by Tom Kolb

Using this no-nonsense book with online audio, guitarists will learn to apply and execute all types of arpeggio forms using a variety of techniques, including alternate picking, sweep picking, tapping, string skipping, and legato.

00695862 Book/Online Audio $19.99

BLUES YOU CAN USE

by John Ganapes

This comprehensive source for learning blues guitar is designed to develop both your lead and rhythm playing. Includes: 21 complete solos • blues chords, progressions and riffs • turnarounds • movable scales and soloing techniques • string bending • utilizing the entire fingerboard • and more.

00142420 Book/Online Media...................................$19.99

CONNECTING PENTATONIC PATTERNS
INCLUDES TAB

by Tom Kolb

If you've been finding yourself trapped in the pentatonic box, this book is for you! This hands-on book with online audio offers examples for guitar players of all levels, from beginner to advanced. Study this book faithfully, and soon you'll be soloing all over the neck with the greatest of ease.

00696445 Book/Online Audio $19.99

FRETBOARD MASTERY
INCLUDES TAB

by Troy Stetina

Untangle the mysterious regions of the guitar fretboard and unlock your potential. This book familiarizes you with all the shapes you need to know by applying them in real musical examples, thereby reinforcing and reaffirming your newfound knowledge.

00695331 Book/Online Audio $19.99

GUITAR AEROBICS
INCLUDES TAB

by Troy Nelson

Here is a daily dose of guitar "vitamins" to keep your chops fine tuned! Musical styles include rock, blues, jazz, metal, country, and funk. Techniques taught include alternate picking, arpeggios, sweep picking, string skipping, legato, string bending, and rhythm guitar.

00695946 Book/Online Audio $19.99

GUITAR CLUES
INCLUDES TAB

OPERATION PENTATONIC

by Greg Koch

Whether you're new to improvising or have been doing it for a while, this book/audio pack will provide loads of delicious licks and tricks that you can use right away, from volume swells and chicken pickin' to intervallic and chordal ideas.

00695827 Book/Online Audio $19.99

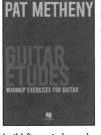

PAT METHENY – GUITAR ETUDES
INCLUDES TAB

Over the years, in many master classes and workshops around the world, Pat has demonstrated the kind of daily workout he puts himself through. This book includes a collection of 14 guitar etudes he created to help you limber up, improve picking technique and build finger independence.

00696587...$15.99

PICTURE CHORD ENCYCLOPEDIA

This comprehensive guitar chord resource for all playing styles and levels features five voicings of 44 chord qualities for all twelve keys – 2,640 chords in all! For each, there is a clearly illustrated chord frame, as well as *an actual photo* of the chord being played!.

00695224...$19.99

RHYTHM GUITAR 365
INCLUDES TAB

by Troy Nelson

This book provides 365 exercises – one for every day of the year! – to keep your rhythm chops fine tuned. Topics covered include: chord theory; the fundamentals of rhythm; fingerpicking; strum patterns; diatonic and non-diatonic progressions; triads; major and minor keys; and more.

00103627 Book/Online Audio $24.99

SCALE CHORD RELATIONSHIPS
INCLUDES TAB

by Michael Mueller & Jeff Schroedl

This book/audio pack explains how to: recognize keys • analyze chord progressions • use the modes • play over nondiatonic harmony • use harmonic and melodic minor scales • use symmetrical scales • incorporate exotic scales • and much more!

00695563 Book/Online Audio $14.99

SPEED MECHANICS FOR LEAD GUITAR
INCLUDES TAB

by Troy Stetina

Take your playing to the stratosphere with this advanced lead book which will help you develop speed and precision in today's explosive playing styles. Learn the fastest ways to achieve speed and control, secrets to make your practice time really count, and how to open your ears and make your musical ideas more solid and tangible.

00699323 Book/Online Audio $19.99

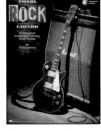

TOTAL ROCK GUITAR
INCLUDES TAB

by Troy Stetina

This comprehensive source for learning rock guitar is designed to develop both lead and rhythm playing. It covers: getting a tone that rocks • open chords, power chords and barre chords • riffs, scales and licks • string bending, strumming, and harmonics • and more.

00695246 Book/Online Audio $19.99

Guitar World Presents
INCLUDES TAB

STEVE VAI'S GUITAR WORKOUT

In this book, Steve Vai reveals his path to virtuoso enlightenment with two challenging guitar workouts – one 10-hour and one 30-hour – which include scale and chord exercises, ear training, sight-reading, music theory, and much more.

00119643...$14.99

HAL•LEONARD®

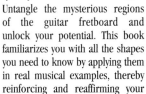

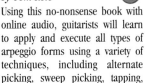
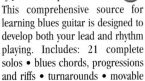
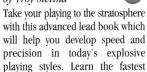
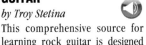